A COMPARATIVE LITERARY STUDY OF DANIEL AND REVELATION

Shaping the End

A COMPARATIVE LITERARY STUDY
OF DANIEL AND REVELATION

Shaping the End

James H. Sims

MELLEN BIBLICAL PRESS
Lewiston/Queenston/Lampeter

Library of Congress Cataloging-in-Publication Data

Sims, James H.
    A comparative literary study of Daniel and Revelation : shaping
the end / James H. Sims.
        p.   cm.
    Includes bibliographical references and index.
    ISBN 0-7734-2361-3
    1. Bible. O.T. Daniel--Criticism, interpretation, etc.
    2. Bible. N.T. Revelation--Criticism, interpretation, etc.
    I. Title.
    BS1555.2.S54 1994
    224'.5066--dc20   94-26154
                                                                 CIP

A CIP catalog record for this book is available from the British Library.

All rights reserved. For information contact

The Edwin Mellen Press   The Edwin Mellen Press
        Box 450   Box 67
Lewiston, New York   Queenston, Ontario
    USA 14092-0450   CANADA L0S 1L0

The Edwin Mellen Press, Ltd.
Lampeter, Dyfed, Wales
UNITED KINGDOM SA48 7DY

Printed in the United States of America

FOR ELIZABETH

γυνὴ περιβεβλημένη

τὸν ἥλιον

CONTENTS

PART III: DANIEL AND REVELATION

PART IV: PERSONAL AFTERWORD

PREFACE

This book takes its origin from another, larger one that I have yet to complete; though much of it is in draft form, more of it is in my mind, and the whole project has seen alternating periods of stasis and forward movement for almost two decades—more of the former than the latter for several years now because of a detour into the realm of academic administration. The book when completed will be entitled, perhaps, ''The Shape of Scripture'' and will offer a literary analysis of the Hebrew Scriptures and the Apocrypha. The present volume is the result of several actions, each of which led to others. The first was to extract from the book manuscript an article on the major literary prophets which appeared in the *Dalhousie Review* in 1981 and evoked correspondence from several scholars, especially the section on the Book of Daniel. The second was my acceptance of an invitation from Leland Ryken to rework and expand the Daniel material in that essay into a chapter for his and Tremper Longman III's *A Complete Literary Guide to the Bible* (Zondervan, 1993). The third was my far exceeding the limitations of length specified for the chapter and my reluctance to discard any of it. I did, however, reduce the Daniel material for the Ryken-Longman book (and here gratefully acknowledge their and the publisher's permission to publish it in this much enhanced form). The fourth action was to combine in one book a literary analysis of the Bible's two apocalypses, Daniel and Revelation. To do this was not an easy decision; in fact I had steadfastly avoided writing on any of the New Testament books, most particularly Revelation (for reasons I attempt to explain in the Personal Afterword at the end of this volume), and I wanted to complete the projected literary study of the Old Testament without engagement in the New Testament.

The more I reviewed the literature on Daniel and Revelation, however, the more the conviction grew that such a book as this should be written by someone. The few book-length studies which consider both Daniel and Revelation deal with the two apocalypses as parallel phenomena but not as works intertextually connected except by references and allusions in the latter to the former. Reading the apocalyptic texts of Daniel and John, I saw many more interrelationships than, to my knowledge, had been commented on by others. As I have learned a great deal about both books from the works of so many who have gone before me, so I hope that my observations will be of interest to others who follow me, whether they find grounds in their own study for confirmation of or disagreement with my analyses.

I wish to express my gratitude to the directors and staff members of particular libraries in which I have spent many hours as a reader: The Henry E. Huntington Library, The Joseph Cook Library of the University of Southern Mississippi, The Newberry Library, The John T. Christian Library of the New Orleans Baptist Theological Seminary, and The Howard Tilton Library of Tulane university. My special thanks go to Karolyn Thompson of the Cook Library for her invaluable assistance in borrowing materials from university and seminary libraries too numerous to list here.

To my students in literary study of the Bible classes over many years, both at the University of Oklahoma and the University of Southern Mississippi, I owe much for their patience with my discurses on, at times, rather esoteric matters and for their insightful and often inspiring questions and comments. I thank also the faculty and students of the Department of English at Wheaton College for allowing me to test some of my ideas against theirs in discussions at that institution in 1991-92 while I was serving as Clyde Kilby Lecturer.

The encouragingly helpful criticism of Leland Ryken, Tremper Longman III, William B. Hunter, Jr., Noel Polk, and Ita Sheres is acknowledged with thanks, though since I did not always follow their suggestions, they share no blame for any errors of fact or conclusion.

Two great men, who now "rest from their labors [and whose] works [have] follow[ed] them," deserve grateful mention for their kindness as mentors and their consistency in providing examples of scholarly excellence in biblical criticism: John Paul Pritchard and Samuel Sandmel. To the most important person in my life because of her unselfish encouragement, steadfast love, and infectious joy I have dedicated this book.

PART I
DANIEL

[God] revealeth the deep and secret things:
he knoweth what is in the darkness,
and the light dwelleth with him.

(Daniel 2:22)

Introduction

The Book of Daniel is perpetually fascinating to readers, primarily perhaps because of its mysterious nature. It combines tautly dramatic narratives with a historically factual tone in its first half and uses vividly enigmatic visions to portray a certain and hope-filled future in which Israel's enemies are suddenly destroyed by divine intervention in its second half. Yet Chapters 7 through 12 reflect largely historical events in visionary form swirling around the same hero as the young man at the center of the narratives in Chapters 1 through 6, in three of which he foresees calamities to be divinely visited upon godless rulers and regimes to vindicate the faith in God of his people.

Thus the book displays a unity of theme, character, and imagery that counterbalances the seeming disparity of its two parts. The chief protagonist appears to be the same righteous man paralleled with Noah and Job in Ezekiel 14:14 and praised as the knower of dark secrets in Ezekiel 28:3, but he is no less mysterious, indeed he is more so, for these brief references. Like the Daniel of the Apocryphal Song of the Three, Susanna, and Bel and the Dragon, Ezekiel's Daniel is noted for righteousness and practical wisdom, not for seeing and interpreting apocalyptic visions. Yet the Daniel of the book that bears his name clearly exhibits the more pragmatic virtues of Ezekiel's and the Apocrypha's Daniel, though he is most fully developed as a divine, while still a very human, seer.

While the following literary analysis of the Book of Daniel may serve to increase some of the mysteries of the work rather than to solve them, its intention is to bring into clear focus some of the light already shed by others on the book's form and historicity as well as on its unity and effectiveness as literature: my hope is that this study will also provide some new light on these important subjects.

Chapter 1

Genre, Chronology, and Historicity

Genre

Daniel is not included with the prophets (nebi'im) in the Jewish Tanak but with the miscellaneous "writings" (ketubim), between the books of Esther and Ezra-Nehemiah. In most Christian Bibles, however, the Book of Daniel is grouped among the prophets, although its distinctively separate narrative section, its unconditional predictions of the end-time coupled with what appear to be specific though "sealed" time-tables, and its full-blown apocalypticism are recognized by most Christian scholars as features that make it unlike the books of the prophets. Perhaps the primary reason for the book's exclusion by the Jews from the prophetic books is the late date for its promulgation, since it came into circulation after prophecy was believed to have ceased. According to the Talmud, the men of the "Great Synagogue," including Haggai, Zechariah, and Malachi, wrote (the word probably means compiled or edited from writings transcribed from an earlier oral tradition) both the books of Daniel and Ezekiel: the traditional belief that only in the holy land could Scripture be written required that prophets who spoke and wrote in exile outside the land must have their works written within Israel and Judah. The final form of Daniel, then, would have been reached between 450 and 400 B. C., even if its composition occurred as early as the sixth century, contemporary with Daniel's career in Babylon (Slotki, "Introduction"). The modern consensus of Biblical scholarship determines a date much later, about 165

B. C. (Eissfeldt 520-522), and, according to one critic, the book is not only not prophetic literature, "its hero [is not] to be counted among the prophets of the Old Testament tradition" (Newsome 214). In *The Hebrew Scriptures,* however, Samuel Sandmel discusses Daniel "with the Prophets because the book is more nearly related to them than to the Hagiographa [the writings], which are a heterogeneous collection" (226). Certainly the Book of Daniel has more affinity with the literary prophets than with apocryphal and intertestamental apocalypses; while there is no immediate national crisis occasioning the visions and predictions and no conditions specified within which judgment may be avoided, there is the concern shared by all the Hebrew prophets with the long-range destiny of God's people and the same stress on the individual Jew's responsibility to conduct himself appropriately during times that try men's souls, times of oppression and persecution. It may be that, as Norman Porteous has argued, "certain of the alleged differences between the Book of Daniel and the great prophets of Israel are actually developments of the prophetic teaching adapted to a later time" (Porteous 15).

Many prefer, following the principles of form criticism, to categorize Daniel as an apocalypse that should be grouped with books like Enoch, 2 Esdras, the Assumption of Moses, the Testaments of the Twelve Patriarchs, Baruch (both Syriac and Greek), and Jubilees (Collins, *Apocalyptic Imagination;* Rowland; Kvanvig, *Roots;* Robert Wilson). One critic who agrees explains *apocalypse* as a "sub-type of the larger literary category of eschatology" and sees in Daniel "*eschatology . . . dramatically amplified in a cosmic direction*" (Towner 10-11, italics his), quoting an epigram from Herman Gunkel: "Apocalyptic is . . . mythological eschatology" (12).

Opposing what he considers a consensus among early twentieth-century scholars that "most biblical apocalyptic [was] a foreign import which did not originally grow on Israelite soil" (80), Robert Wilson hypothesizes "apocalyptic groups [whose] social and religious background [determine] the *shape* of [their] religion and literature'' (93, italics his), and he urges that more attention be given to the anthropological evidence about such groups. Since the only available material is in the biblical texts, his proposal amounts to a plea to view the Book of Daniel as self-verifying evidence of a native Hebrew tradition of apocalyptic in much the same way as the Qumran scrolls reveal ''an almost archetypal apocalyptic community'' (80), though he notes that even the Qumran evidence has been accommodated to the standard view of explaining late literary developments as resulting from Persian influence.[1] But whether apocalyptic is a sub-genre of eschatology, as Towner suggests, or a native Hebrew development born of oppressive domination and the need to provide a program for coping, as Robert Wilson argues, or whether it is simply a phenomenon which Israel shares with Persian, Akkadian, and other near-Eastern cultures, the term *apocalyptic* is the most widely used and agreed-upon genre for the Book of Daniel.

There is no necessary contradiction, however, in designating Daniel as both *prophecy* and *apocalypse*, since earlier books of prophecy include such apocalyptic characteristics as the oracular view that history is governed by God and will be brought to its end in such a way as to manifest clearly those who are God's people and those who are his and his people's enemies and visions filled with bizarre and frightening images, sometimes explained with divine help by the prophet and sometimes interpreted to the prophet by supernatural beings (e. g., Ezekiel 1-2, 8, and 38-39, Zechariah 1-8 and 12-14, Joel 3, Isaiah 6 and 24-27).

Chronology and Historicity

The organization and handling of time in the Book of Daniel are particularly interesting and puzzling. Beginning as though a straightforward chronological sequence will be followed, keying events to certain years of certain kings' reigns, the book from its opening verse raises serious questions about its own chronology, questions that the author could not have been blind to. Indeed the writer seems deliberately to invite questions and yet withhold any answers.

And in the book's second half (Chapters 7-12), the events apocalyptically portrayed as predictions are essentially accurate history in proper chronological order, a fact noted early by Porphyry, the third-century neo-Platonic philosopher, who argued for a second-century date for Daniel on this basis (Collins, *Apocalyptic Imagination* 69). To return to the beginning, Daniel 1:1 states that Nebuchadnezzar besieged Jerusalem and captured Judah's king in "the third year of the reign of Jehoiakim," while 2 Kings 24 reports that Jehoiakim was dead and that his son, Jehoiachin, was in already the eighth year of his reign when Nebuchadnezzar took him and "all the treasures of the house of the LORD" to Babylon (24:8-15). Surely an author who knew Jeremiah's prophecies so well (Daniel 9:2, Jeremiah 25:11, 29:10) must have also known the principal characters and time periods of the Kings account. Events as traumatic and with such extensive ramifications for the nation as the siege of Jerusalem and the first exile of Jehoiachin and the cream of Israel's youth, especially since these events were harbingers of the destruction of both the Temple and the Holy City in 586 B. C., could hardly be inaccurately represented without both author and reader recognizing the discrepancies. To place Nebuchadnezzar's (more accurately spelled Nebuchadrezzar's) capture of Jehoiachin and many of the nobility in "the third year of the reign of Jehoiakim" when the events had actually taken place after Jehoiakim's death following an eleven-year reign is as though a modern writer opened a book about an American in a Japanese prisoner-of-war camp with a reference to the attack on Pearl Harbor as having occurred during the presidency of Herbert Hoover. And if the writer then went on to predict in substantially accurate detail the war in Korea and the political atmosphere surrounding it, including President Truman's recall of General MacArthur for pressing the war too far into enemy territory, even though such details were clothed in apocalyptic symbolism, especially if the book did not come to light until, say, A. D. 2300, one would assume the account to be an example of *prophetia ex eventu*, history disguised as prophecy.

In such a circumstance, the most baffling mystery would be, why, even though the accurate history is veiled in apocalyptic symbolism, correctly portray events presented as though in the future following a serious garbling of past events and persons? Would an author wish to be charged with careless anachronism or ignorance? At exactly those points where he transcends history and wishes to be taken seriously as a seer of the future, has he not, by inaccuracies and inconsistencies in reporting past events, achieved the opposite effect, and invited the reader to shrug off the message he considered so vital?

Even so fine a scholar as Samuel Sandmel, with a deep appreciation of the perennial value of the scriptures generally, comments after considering just such problems as discussed here, that the Book of Daniel, in spite of its "edifying tales in the first half of the Book [is so flawed in its attempt at prediction that it] can have little more than an antiquarian interest for us" (238); i.e., there is no continuing relevance of Daniel as apocalyptic. Sandmel is disagreeing with H. H. Rowley, who had argued that in spite of the mistakes of apocalyptists, their predictions show "a sound instinct [and they see] more that is fundamentally true than all that is false" (Rowley 152). Whereas Sandmel accepts the narratives as relevant but not the visions, another writer seems to see the apocalyptic section as the more relevant material and the stories as merely "prefacing the . . . visions" (Birch 28). Helge Kvanvig continues to argue convincingly, however, for the essential relevance of apocalyptic, particularly Daniel, for our time and for the future ("Relevance of Biblical Visions" 44-46).

To return to the problem of errors in chronology, my analogy between Daniel and a writer on recent American history is perhaps not very apt, but the usual explanation for Daniel's historical inaccuracies, as put forth, for example, by Louis F. Hartman in the Anchor Bible, is unsatisfactory to me, and, as I read between the lines, it seems to be unsatisfactory to him as well. According to Hartman, it is "unfair, not to say impious," to demand factual accuracy of an ancient writer consistent with the "canons of nineteenth- and twentieth-century

critical history in a book whose intent is essentially religious and not historical.''
But he then insists that his exposure of inaccuracies does not ''impugn or even
call into question the sacredness, authority, and inerrancy of the Book of Daniel
which are accepted here without question as truths of Christian faith'' (Hartman
53, 54).

While I, as a literary scholar, prefer to exclude sustained examination of
such questions as ''Did the events recorded really happen?'' and ''Are the dates
of events and the historicity of persons reliable?'' as a Christian interpreter, I
cannot easily sidestep such issues in Daniel.[2] Some of the reasons are: the Book
of Revelation and the epistles of Paul draw heavily upon Daniel's imagery and
prophecies of the end-time (e. g., Revelation 13:1-10 with Daniel 7; 2
Thessalonians 2:1-12 with Daniel 11:31-39); according to the Gospels, Jesus
appears to have read Daniel in his day as legitimate prophecy yet to be fulfilled
(e. g., Mark 13:14-27 with Daniel 7-12); the doctrine of the resurrection, so
central to the Christian gospel, is more clearly stated in Daniel (12:2, 13) than in
any other Hebrew text. Only if the book is dependable as Scripture are these New
Testament texts reliable. Rather, then, than follow Hartman in embracing both
horns of the dilemma—Daniel is inaccurate, yet Daniel is inerrant—I suggest
considering Daniel's ''inaccuracies'' as an integral part of his literary technique.

According to this view, for the sake of artistic effect to emphasize theme,
the writer of Daniel deliberately confuses times and persons in the first half of the
book (1-6), where his explanations of dreams and visions are prompt, perfectly
accurate, and speedily fulfilled, and, just as deliberately, he thinly veils historical
persons and events in apocalyptic metaphors in his substantially accurate second
half (7-12). In this latter half, far from being the confidently poised young wise
man of the narratives, Daniel is troubled and perplexed by his visions; depends on
angelic explicators who never completely satisfy his curiosity (indeed, the most
crucial prophecies are sealed from him and from his readers until some
indeterminate future time); faints, falls ill, and must finally have visions replaced

by angelic narrative (11-12), incapable of sustaining the continued strain of viewing the astounding images first-hand. The writer seems to be setting the two halves of the book against each other in genre (narrative vs. apocalyptic), nature of the protagonist (third-person strong wiseman vs. first-person weak *naif*), and credibility of the work's unity (erroneous history and clearly revealed mysteries are followed by accurate though metaphoric history and mystifyingly incomplete revelations) while, at the same time, skillfully unifying the two halves by, to cite a few examples, connecting themes with diverse imagery (four earthly kingdoms replaced by a divine kingdom in chapters 2 and 7), repeating similar literary forms (a psalm in chapter 2 and a prayer in chapter 9), anticipating the beast-rulers by a ruler-beast (chapters 4 and 7-8), flashing back to past reigns for the timing of visions (chapters 6 and 7-8, 9, and 11), foreshadowing a vision in Cyrus's reign by early references (chapters 1 and 10), and bridging the Hebrew of 1:1-2:4a and 8-12 by the Aramaic of chapters 2:4b-7:28.[3]

The apparently chronological order of the narratives in Chapters 1-6 (the first years of Nebuchadnezzar's reign, Belshazzar's ''reign'' [or Belsharusar's co-regency with Nabonidus, not as successor to Nebuchadnezzar], the reign of Darius, and the reign of Cyrus, ca. 604-485 B. C.) is replaced by the achronological order of the visions in Chapters 7-12 (the early years of Belshazzar, the third year of Cyrus, and the first year of Darius, ca. 530-520 B. C.). Yet this contradictory tension pulling apart the book's two halves, so deliberately developed, is yet powerfully counteracted by unifying devices, as we have seen. Clearly each half shares some features of the other: the narrative half (1-6) includes dream-visions and the visionary half (7-12) includes narrative; indeed, what is commonly referred to as the ''fourth vision,'' Chapters 10-12, is actually a brief vision initiating a long narration.

Commenting on the ''historical blunders'' of the Book of Daniel, Arthur Jeffery remarks that ''to stress . . . that the capture of Jerusalem was not in . . . 606 B. C., but in 597 . . .; that Nebuchadnezzar should be spelled Nebuchadrezzar, that Belshazzar was not his son . . . and was never king;[4] that there is confusion in its order of the Persian kings and a foreshortening of their history [four only are mentioned in Daniel 11:2]; that 'satrap' was not a Babylonian title, and so on, is to fasten on unessentials'' (345). Yet such a statement ignores the prominent position the book's author gives to his "blunders"; Jeffery praises the writer of Daniel for having "caught the conception that history is a whole . . . . in which God's eternal purpose is developing'' (351), though he regards that writer as one with very little grasp of essential matters of chronology and fact that must undergird the whole. The efforts of Jeremiah and Ezekiel, for example, to date their prophecies in relation to historical events show that it is not a uniquely modern view that accurate and judicious marshalling of fact should support an account's credibility, even if that account is in the service of theology or religion. It is true, of course, that the degree of factual accuracy and objectivity modern critical historians have prized (especially in other historians), at least since the mid-nineteenth century, would not have been attempted by an ancient historian, whether Hebrew, Greek, or Roman. But to assume that a writer can be unwittingly so grossly inaccurate as Daniel is alleged to have been (especially when the assumption is coupled with the conviction that Daniel is a production of the first or second century B. C. when an essentially accurate account like that in Maccabees was being written) is to assume a writer who is himself an anachronism—one who not only has a careless attitude toward fact but presumes a similar attitude in an audience steeped already for centuries in a tradition of prophetic utterance embedded in dependable historical fact.

Again, I propose an alternative to such views as those of Hartman and Jeffery. I suggest assuming a careful craftsman whose artistic and theological purpose is usefully served in the early chapters by apparent disregard of chronological order, royal succession, and accurate court nomenclature. The effect on the reader is a reinforcement of the message that Nebuchadnezzar and Belshazzar never really learn: that "the most high God [rules] in the kingdom of men, and *that* he appointeth over it whomsoever he will'' (Daniel 5:21b); i. e., that the true sovereign is God and human rulers pale into insignificance, even disappear as though they had never existed or appear and sit on thrones they never occupied in life, in the great panorama of Yahweh's universal rule. Again, the reader's grasp is made sure on the theme that time, whether represented by divisions of "years" or "weeks" or "times," whether unfolding according to historical memory or creative fancy, is under the control of him whose kingdom "shall stand for ever" (Daniel 2:44); even "what shall come to pass hereafter" (Daniel 2:45b) can be shown by the eternal Lord as though it had already passed.

In Chapter 2 Daniel's psalm speaks of the Lord's sovereign control over both time (as evidenced in nature's flux) and human rulers (whether humanely benevolent, blasphemous and cowardly, or bestially rapacious):

> Blessed be the name of God for ever and ever:
> For wisdom and might are his:
> And he changeth the times and the seasons:
> He removeth kings, and setteth up kings.
> (Daniel 2:20-21a)

Here Daniel directly challenges the fatalism of Babylon's astral religion (Slotki xiv) and asserts that day passes into night, winter to spring, and so on, because of the Lord's constantly sustaining the phenomena of nature, not because of a naturally deterministic universe. Time, both in the blessings and the sorrows it brings, and human kingdoms, whether comparatively gold, silver, or metals of lesser worth, seem to be supremely important from the human point of view, but from the divine overview, both time and principalities are "like the chaff of the summer threshing-floors" (Daniel 2:35), gone with the wind even before they come into being. Thus in a book so filled with significant periods of time and overwhelmingly powerful forces that affect human life—past, present, future—the only abiding reality is God and his mysterious kingdom, the only proper concern of man to be loyal and obedient to him. Regardless of whether or not loyalty and obedience bring temporal deliverance, one may through them triumph over time and worldly pomp (Daniel 3:17-18; 12:1-3). As Lacoque so well expresses it: "Le temps est télescopé dans le moment vécu. . . . L'instant remplit l'horizon. . . il *faut* que vienne un monde nouveau, le monde de Dieu. [Q]uand le Royaume semble le plus éloigné, il est le plus proche" (184, 185).

Chapter 2
Literary Analysis

The Book as a Whole

Whether composed by one author or by such a group as the Great Synagogue working with older materials, the Book of Daniel is a sophisticated literary unit, bound together in a final shape that is aesthetically satisfying, thematically clear, and yet finally open-ended and mysterious.[5]

As we have seen, the Book of Daniel falls rather naturally into two halves (the narratives of chapters 1-6 and the visions of chapters 7-12) but paradoxically maintains its unity as a literary whole by creating both centripetal forces (motifs and images shared by both halves) and centrifugal forces (clear visions and confused history followed by clear history communicated through puzzling visions).[6] The six narratives are virtually self-contained: the same Hebrew characters figure throughout—Daniel and his three friends, Shadrach, Meshach, and Abednego, in Chapters 1 and 2; the three without Daniel in Chapter 3; and Daniel without the three in Chapters 4, 5, and 6—and in each narrative the pagan monarch is centrally important—Nebuchadnezzar in Chapters 1, 2, 3, and 4; Belshazzar in Chapter 5; and Darius in Chapter 6. But despite the continuity of characters from story to story and their chronological order, one narrative never depends on another, though some careful interlinking is evident (e. g., Nebuchadnezzar's bringing vessels from the Jerusalem Temple to Babylon prepares for Belshazzar's sacrilegious feast [Daniel 1:2 with 5:2-4,23] and

Belshazzar is reminded of Nebuchadnezzar's transmogrification [Daniel 4:33 with 5:21]; the "wise *men* of Babylon" fail in divination and interpretation of dreams where Daniel succeeds [Daniel 2:12,24 with 4:18]; Nebuchadnezzar's decree that an image be worshipped is replaced by a decree honoring God, and Darius' decree that no one petition any man or God save him is replaced by a decree honoring God [Daniel 3:4-6, 29 with 6:7-9, 25-27]). Indeed, the lack of explicit narrative links or expository cross-referencing between stories raises some of the puzzling questions which have intrigued modern readers, as they had earlier stimulated the imaginations of rabbinical and Christian commentators: why is Daniel not involved or even mentioned in connection with his three friends' escape from the fiery furnace? Why do the three friends disappear without a trace after their deliverance from the furnace? Why is it that Nebuchadnezzar never seems to learn permanently the superiority of the God of the Jews but continues to act in each story as through he has just for the first time seen proof of God's power? The text does not help one answer such questions of the narratives.

Even though they are not in the chronological sequence of the narratives, the visions of the second part of Daniel are linked by expository narrative (Daniel 7:1,28; 8:1-2, 15-18, 27; 9:1-27; 10:1-4, 7-13). One's first impression in reading Chapters 7-12 is of chronological order because of the opening verses of each chapter (except 12), but upon comparison, one finds that not only does Chapter 7 revert from the reign of Cyrus (6:28) to that of Belshazzar, after Chapters 7-10 have progressed from Belshazzar (7-first year, 8-third year) to Darius (9-first year) to Cyrus (10-third year), Chapter 11 suddenly flashes back to Darius (first year) as Daniel's divine instructor encourages him with the intelligence that he and Michael have carried on their struggle against evil earthly forces all through Daniel's career and will do so until the final triumph of good (12:1). Since the narrator has informed us from the beginning that "Daniel continued *even* unto the first year of king Cyrus" (1:21), why do the final vision and narration begin in the third year of Cyrus (10:1)?

Although "Daniel prospered in the reign of Darius, and in the reign of Cyrus the Persian" (6:28), perhaps Daniel's status as a wise man consulted by successive monarchs came to an end in the first year of Cyrus; if so, his mourning, fasting, and weakness may have resulted in part from his demotion. Such a circumstance may also explain the especially tender concern and complimentary approach of his divine visitor: he is touched, stood upright, addressed as "greatly beloved," and strengthened to receive the final vision-narration (10:2-19). Heaven has continued to work on behalf of the vindication and blessing of the wise like Daniel even though earthly developments give no hint of the coming victory—and Heaven will continue to work until "thy people shall be delivered" (12:1). Danna Fewell, using different textual evidence, argues convincingly that Daniel has political aspirations and is so changed in the last part of the book because, not having been able to sustain his courtly influence as he had done successfully earlier, he fears that ultimate victory will come only after his death (159-160).

The absence of introductory links to bind the six narratives together and the abrupt beginning of each contributes to the reader's impression that these stories constitute a collection of originally independent anecdotes about the intellectual and moral elite of Israel in the courts of pagan kings.[7] The apocryphal stories in the Septuagint are similarly related only by their having to do with Daniel, though those stories are of quite a different generic order; it has even been suggested that Susanna and Bel and the Dragon are early forms of the detective story (Lasine). At any rate, one can understand the narratives of Daniel 1-6, as well as those of the Apocrypha, having been taken as midrashic tales intended to illustrate general truths or abstract principles rather than to relate historical occurrences involving historical personages.

I suggest that in the narratives of Daniel 1-6 we have stories intended to be received as historical events involving actual persons and places but that what was much more important to the author than convincing historicity was an artistic arrangement calculated to give maximum effect to the moral and theological message embodied in the stories.[8] The very deliberate sequencing of the narratives reflects Daniel's and his friends' growth in the knowledge of the Lord, the effectiveness of worshipping him in pagan surroundings, and an awareness of the involvement of Yahweh in the direction of the whole world; by extension, through these stories, any faithful believer is encouraged to grow through loyalty and obedience in these areas of thought, devotion, and influence.

Seen in this light, the six narratives constitute six oppositions of the human and the divine with the divine always triumphing and the human beings either recognizing and rejoicing in that triumph or being destroyed by their failure to acknowledge it. Each story builds on the effect of the preceding one; the visions of Chapters 7-12 further illustrate and extend into the future and throughout the cosmos the lessons learned.

The young Hebrews learn, or test their prior knowledge of, the superiority of divine over human nurture (Chapter 1) leading to the gift of superior wisdom (1:17); this divine wisdom exemplified in Daniel himself (Chapter 2) soon triumphs over the combined wisdom of Babylon's sages of whatever school (2:27-28); such wisdom, now exemplified in the three friends (Chapter 3), dictates their willingness to die for the worship of the true God rather than to participate in idolatrous worship, no matter how grandly staged and enforced by earthly power (3:14, 16-18). Divine nurture, divine wisdom, and divine worship are further developed into recognition of divine sovereignty (Chapter 4) and the dependence upon it of human rule (4:25), of the divine judgment on blasphemous kings who fail to acknowledge that dependence (Chapter 5), and of divine deliverance for the faithful and divine destruction for their malicious enemies (Chapter 6).

These last divine manifestations of sovereignty, judgment, and deliverance, having been so effectively proclaimed in story, are next illustrated in the visions of the four kingdoms (Chapter 7) and an even more startling view of the fourth kingdom (Chapter 8). Divine nurture from the Scriptures now leads to wisdom enabling Daniel to understand Jeremiah's past prophecy of the seventy weeks and to prophesy the future seventy sevens of years (weeks), the last seven years (one week) to be projected beyond history's horizon (Chapter 9). Daniel's final revelations (Chapters 10, 11, 12) come after a period of abstinence from all human, physical nurture (10:2-3); yet the divine, spiritual nurture of a vision very like Ezekiel's (Daniel 10:4-6, 10; Ezekiel 1:26-2:2) brings supernatural strength (10:18-19) and wisdom (10:21) to receive a view of the distant future. Though not to be fully understood by Daniel, and therefore neither by the reader, the prophetic foreview of Chapters 10-12 illustrates divine rule, judgment, and deliverance (reminiscent of Chapters 4-6); the perversion of divine worship into blasphemy (11:36-39); and judgment on the wicked and deliverance for the righteous, even for those who have died, all brought about by the Lord who alone rules not only the world's history but the cosmos (12:1-3, 10-13).

The tabulation on page 20 represents the relationship of parts to the whole of Daniel as perceived in the foregoing discussion.

The Book of Daniel

The Six Narratives   The Four Visions

Ch. Theme   Ch. Theme

1 Divine vs. Human Nurture

2 Divine vs. Human Wisdom & Rule

3 Divine vs. Human Worship

4 Divine vs. Human Rule

5 Divine vs. Human Judgment

6 Divine vs. Human Deliverance

                                      7 Four Kingdoms: Vanity of Human Rule & Judgment; Divine Deliverance

8 Fourth Kingdom: Vanity of Human Rule & Judgment; Divine Deliverance

9 Divine Nurture (Word) Brings Light

10 Divine Nurture (Prayer) Brings Divine Wisdom & Strength

11 Divine Wisdom Brings Prescience

12 Divine Judgment & Deliverance are Sure; When & How are Sealed

Chapter 3
The Narratives (Chapters 1-6)

one

Of many young Jewish captives taken to Babylon for special learning only Daniel (renamed Belteshazzar by his captors), Hananiah (Shadrach), Mishael (Meshach), and Azariah (Abednego) are memorialized in the Hebrew Scriptures. Isaiah had prophesied to Hezekiah, who had shown Babylonian emissaries all his treasures, that when Babylon conquered Jerusalem such would be the fate of all of the princely blood who survived the fall of the kingdom of Judah.

> Hear the word of the LORD. Behold, the days come that all that *is* in thine house, and that which thy fathers have laid up in store unto this day, shall be carried unto Babylon: nothing shall be left, saith the LORD. And of thy sons that shall issue from thee, which thou shalt beget, shall they take away; and they shall be eunuchs in the palace of the king of Babylon.
>
> (2 Kings 20:17-18; cf. Isaiah 39:5-7)

Hezekiah's response strikes the reader as shockingly self-centered: "Good *is* the word of the LORD which thou hast spoken. . . *Is it* not *good*, if peace and truth be in my days?" (2 Kings 20:19). A passage in Isaiah has been seen as a prophecy of the careers of Daniel and his three friends[9] because of the emphasis upon those who choose what pleases God and hold fast to his holy covenant, virtues which characterize the young men throughout the Book of Daniel (considering Daniel as representative of the four even when three are absent), but especially in Chapters 1, 3, 6, and 9.

> Neither let the eunuch say, Behold, I *am* a dry tree. For thus saith the
> LORD unto the eunuchs that keep my sabbaths, and choose *the things*
> that please me, and take hold of my covenant; even unto them will I give
> in mine house and within my walls a place and a name better than of
> sons and of daughters: I will give them an everlasting name, that shall not
> be cut off [a name imperishable for all time, NEB].
>
> (Isaiah 56:3b-5)

The first narrative sets the stage for the entire book, both narratives and visions, by describing Daniel and his friends as young men of unblemished physique, attractive personality, high intelligence, and eagerness for learning. Above all, with Daniel leading the way, they are young men of unquestioning loyalty to Yahweh and the law of Moses; they are all rewarded with wisdom and aptitude for learning beyond that of human beings untouched by God's grace, and Daniel in particular is given "understanding in all visions and dreams" (Daniel 1:17), a gift he will have ample opportunity to exercise. Although Daniel is their leader-spokesman, all four youths star in the first story as their plain, vegetarian diet results in better health and handsomer appearance than all those who partake of the king's food and drink, rich nourishment that, under ordinary circumstances, would easily give its partakers the advantage of "fairer and fatter . . . flesh" (1:15). But these circumstances are decidedly extraordinary. Concerned lest portions of the king's provisions have been offered to idols, Daniel "purpose[s] in his heart" not to defile himself, and Melzar, the chief eunuch, after a brief testing period to insure that his charges will not so fade away as to endanger his own health and life, allows the four friends to eat only vegetables (probably rice or other cereals). At the end of the testing period, not only do the friends give a better appearance than any others in their group, their wisdom and understanding are so advanced that Nebuchadnezzar finds them "ten times better than all the magicians *and* astrologers that *were* in his realm'' (1:20), foreshadowing the superiority demonstrated later (2:27-28, 4:18-25, and 5:8, 25).

two

The young Hebrews, then, have all proved themselves steadfast in observing dietary prohibitions and in enhanced wisdom. Now, in the second narrative, Daniel proves himself through complete dependence on the Lord a true interpreter of visions and dreams, anticipating the fourth and fifth narratives and even to some degree the last half of the book. As are all the narratives, the second story is effectively told in a style appropriate to its theme; the space given to Nebuchadnezzar's unreasonable demand that his magicians both recover and interpret his forgotten dream and their insistence that only ''the gods, whose dwelling is not with flesh'' (2:11) could do such a thing heightens the effect of Daniel's success, the nature of Yahweh in responding to prayers of all the young men (2:17-19) to assure that success, and the concern of Daniel that God, not he, get all the credit for the ·revelation (literally, the apocalypse). His psalm of thanksgiving for the revelation of the ''night vision'' (2:19-23), Arioch's great relief that the threat of death will not be carried out against the wise ones (2:24-25), and Nebuchadnezzar's acknowledgment that the God of the Jews is superior not only over kings and their secrets but also over other gods (2:47)—all these provide appropriate preparation for the most striking figure of all, the symbol of God's everlasting kingdom destined to supersede all temporal kingdoms, as represented by a man's image in various metals, when their declining history has run its course:

> and the stone that smote the image became a great mountain, and filled
> the whole earth. . . . the dream *is* certain, and the interpretation thereof
> sure.
>
> (Daniel 2:35b, 45b)

three

In the third narrative, as though Nebuchadnezzar had become obsessed with Daniel's identification of him as the "head of gold" in the great image of his dream (2:38) and was determined to refashion the entire image in gold and thus assure the continuance of his reign, he sets up an enormous statue of gold and decrees that all must fall down and worship the image at the sound of orchestral music; all who fail to worship are to be destroyed in a blazing furnace (3:1-6). But a furnace heated seven times beyond its customary temperature cannot so much as singe the hair of God's servants, who believe their God can deliver them, but are ready to die anyway rather than worship an idol if God does not deliver them (3:18). The third repetition of the king's "princes, governors, and captains, and the king's counselors" (3:27) is in the context, not of their awe at the golden image as formerly, but of their astonishment that "the fire had no power [over the Hebrews], nor was a hair of their head singed, neither were their coats changed, nor the smell of fire had passed on them" (3:27).

The thrice-repeated list of governmental dignitaries gathered at the dedication ceremony and the four-times-repeated catalogue of musical instruments in the orchestra mock the ridiculous vanity of human pomp over against the sublime simplicity of the Lord, who delivers his faithful worshippers from the furnace by sending only one "angel," one who, though "like the Son of God," appears secretly and disappears silently (3:25, 28). The mockery of human sovereignty (supposed) is also reinforced by the twelve-times repeated catalogue of the Babylonian names of the heroes of the story; "Shadrach, Meshach, and Abednego" not only show the power of their God in faith and obedience, but the narrator himself, and even Nebuchadnezzar the king (3:14,26,28-29; four times), pay ironic tribute to their courage to resist pagan practices by using their Babylonian names: though their names have been changed, their Jewishness remains. Nebuchadnezzar is made the mouthpiece to celebrate the God-centered faith of the young men and thus to highlight the theme of the story:

> Blessed *be* the God of Shadrach, Meshach, and Abednego, who hath sent his angel, and delivered his servants that trusted in him, and have changed the king's word, and yielded their bodies, that they might not serve nor worship any god, except their own God.
>
> (Daniel 3:28)

After this, that Nebuchadnezzar presumes to protect the reputation of such a powerful God by his kingly decree (3:29) is perhaps the supreme irony of the story.

four

The structure of the fourth narrative (Chapter 4) is uniquely appropriate to its subject, the divine rule of Yahweh who presides over all kings and kingdoms, since Nebuchadnezzar's dream of humiliation—including the images of the tree cut down and the ruler reduced to bestiality—is self-narrated; Daniel's interpretation and the dream's fulfillment is then narrated in the usual mode of Chapters 1-6 with the king and Daniel viewed as third-person characters; and finally, Nebuchadnezzar's recognition of God as truly sovereign and his restoration to sanity and his throne is told in first-person narration by the king himself.[10] The shifts in point of view are especially effective: the king's obliviousness to his own pride as he narrates the dream, Daniel's sympathetic and troubled hesitation in interpreting the dream followed by the description of the nadir of Nebuchadnezzar's fall, and the suddenness of the king's restoration at the end of the seven years are more affectingly responded to because of the psychological immediacy of the first and third sections and the distancing of the second.

The fourth narrative begins with a prologue, spoken by Nebuchadnezzar himself, expressing the theme of the Lord's sovereignty throughout eternity and over all the earth.

> How great *are* [the Lord's] signs!
> And how mighty *are* his wonders!
> His kingdom is an everlasting kingdom,
> And his dominion is from generation to generation.
> (Daniel 4:3; Hebrew 3:33)[11]

The king's narration of his troubling dream of himself as a mighty tree, "strong [with its] height . . . reach[ing] unto heaven, and the sight thereof to the end of all the earth" (4:11), cut down by command of "a watcher . . . from heaven," includes a strikingly personal statement of this theme in the loud cry of heaven's holy one:

> that the living may know that the most High ruleth in the kingdom of men, and giveth it to whomsoever he will, and setteth up over it the basest of men.   (Daniel 4:17b)[12]

That he is the ruler to be changed to the form of a beast for seven years apparently does not initially occur to Nebuchadnezzar, though he doubtless identifies himself with the glorious, universal tree which protects and provides for all the earth's life. After all, the earlier dream (Chapter 2) had identified him as the head of gold, and not his own but kingdoms several times removed from his are the ones to be destroyed. The reader, however, anticipates Daniel's application of the humiliation as well as the glory to Nebuchadnezzar; perhaps the Babylonian wise men also anticipate it. If so, their failure to interpret the dream may result as much from fear as from inability; even Daniel is cautiously courteous and hesitant to apply such a devastating prophecy to the powerful king (4:19).

Daniel's characteristically forthright courage asserts itself as he pronounces God's judgment, however, and his peroration is almost as daring as his stern reprimand of Belshazzar in the following narrative (5:23), implying as it does that the king has been less than a fruitful tree to many of his subjects: "O king, let my counsel be acceptable unto thee, and break off thy sins by righteousness, and thine iniquities by showing mercy to the poor; if it may be a lengthening of thy tranquility" (4:27). Daniel holds out no hope of reprieve from the dream's judgment, only a delay; that the humiliation of Nebuchadnezzar comes twelve months later may suggest that the king did walk more humbly and rule more justly for a while. At year's end, however, when his characteristic pride asserts itself, within that same hour he is reduced to bestial form and mind and driven from human society for seven years.

> Nebuchadnezzar . . . was driven from men, and did eat grass as oxen, and his body was wet with the dew of heaven, till his hairs were grown like eagles' *feathers,* and his nails like birds' *claws* .
>
> (Daniel 4:33)

The anomalous nature of Nebuchadnezzar's bestial form anticipates the beast-rulers of the apocalyptic section of Daniel (Chapters 7 and 8; see Burkholder 48 and Rosenberg 450-451),[13] underscoring in the later chapters of Daniel the control God exercises over human kingdoms to accomplish his purposes, a theme sounded from the second verse of the book: "the LORD gave Jehoiakim king of Judah into [Nebuchadnezzar's] hand." Kings view their actions as autonomously willed; Daniel reveals them as willed by God: "the most High ruleth in the kingdom of men, and giveth it to whomsoever he will, and setteth up over it the basest of men" (4:17,25); "he doeth according to his will in the army of heaven, and *among* the inhabitants of the earth: and none can stay his hand, or say unto him, What doest thou?" (4:35). Stated by the narrator, by Daniel, and by Nebuchadnezzar, this theme "does not suggest a fickle sovereignty, however; it is put in the context of the final doxology, which notes: 'his promises are always faithfully fulfilled, his ways are always just' (v. 37)" (Burkholder 51).

five

The fifth narrative emphasizes that Belshazzar has not profited from his predecessor's example as Daniel repeats to him the story of Nebuchadnezzar's brutal transformation (5:20-22). In spite of the connective allusion, however, this narrative has a theme and a method of communicating it quite different from the fourth. The contrast now is between human judgment among values and divine judgment. Belshazzar's distorted sense of value is shown not only by his using in a drunken feast the holy vessels from the Temple of a God his predecessor had learned to respect and fear, if not worship, but also by his apparently having forgotten until reminded by the queen that the one wise man who had correctly interpreted mysteries for the previous king is still in his court. Furthermore, he considers expensive clothes, jewelry, and political position as the most attractive rewards one can offer; indeed, after Daniel has explained the apparition of the writing hand as having sealed Belshazzar's fate, Belshazzar persists in proclaiming Daniel "third ruler" in a kingdom that cannot endure until the next sunrise (5:24-31). On the other hand, Daniel illustrates one whose sense of values is guided by divine judgment; he learns well and remembers the lessons of history (5:18-21), distinguishes between empty materialism and the self-rewarding satisfaction of serving God, and is a voluntary spokesman for and interpreter of his God, not a mercenary soothsayer.

> Let thy gifts be to thy self, and give thy rewards to another; yet I will read the writing unto the king and make known unto him the interpretation.
>
> (Daniel 5:17)

The writing, described early in the story (5:5-8) but revealed in meaning very near the end, is "MENE, MENE, TEKEL, UPHARSIN," which Daniel interprets as: MENE; God hath numbered thy kingdom, and finished it. TEKEL; Thou art weighed in the balances, and art found wanting. PERES; Thy kingdom is divided, and given to the Medes and Persians.

> (Daniel 5:26-28)

The theme of accurate judgment of value from the divine perspective is well brought out by the mysterious words; they are names of coins, arranged in descending order of value as the great image of Chapter 2 was composed of metals of descending worth from head to foot. *"Mene, mene, tekel, u-pharsin:*

tekel, Heb. *shekel*, was a sixtieth of a *mene*, Heb. *mina*. *U* means 'and'; *pharsin* means two *pheres*, with one *pheres* being a half-shekel'' (Daniel 5:25, NEB note). The kingdom of Babylon, then, under Nebuchadnezzar, though a ''head of gold'' (2:38), was only comparatively better than those who followed, as Belshazzar is the most lightweight monarch in a succession of pieces of small change. The Lord of the universe, who weighs all earthly things in his just scales (Isaiah 26:7, 40:12; Job 31:6), has found Belshazzar and his kingdom unable to measure up even to the inferior standards of his predecessors; therefore, his kingdom has already been consigned to the Persians. Perhaps the image of weighing in scales here suggested the Talmud's comment, ''if [Daniel] were placed in one scale of the balance and all the wisest heathens in the other, he would have outweighed them'' (Slotki xi, citing Yoma 77a). Certain it is that this image and its context are conflated with classical allusions in Milton's *Paradise Lost*, Book IV, when Gabriel points out to Satan that he is too light in God's scales (seen in the constellation Libra) to fight against Eden's angelic guard (Sims 178-179; Rosenberg 449).

Among the narratives in Daniel, the fifth is unique in including a woman as character, and she is an essential character at that. Without the queen (identified as the ''queen-mother'' in NRSV, OT 1135), Belshazzar's and the kingdom's destruction would have come without warning, since she calls Daniel and his divine gift of interpretation to Belshazzar's attention; thus the queen is a *sine qua non* for one of the most memorable of the narratives of the book. As a poised and confident rememberer of valuable knowledge, she serves as a foil to Belshazzar's ludicrous figure of the drunken coward with his blanched countenance, loosened loins, and knocking knees (5:6-9) who has forgotten Daniel and his relationship with Nebuchadnezzar. The queen's portrayal of Daniel is the most glowing description of him in the Book of Daniel, perhaps hinting that she too has had the benefit of his revelatory gift: he possesses ''the spirit of the holy gods . . the wisdom of the gods . . . an excellent spirit, and knowledge, and understanding,'' and he can interpret dreams, solve enigmas, and unravel difficulties (5:11-12). Her speech begins and ends in supreme confidence: "Let not thy thoughts trouble thee, there is a man—" (5:10-11); "let Daniel be called, and he will show the interpretation" (5:12). As a character she highlights Belshazzar's ineptness as ruler, since he apparently does not remember a man still in his kingdom who was so important to Nebuchadnezzar that he appointed him "master of the magicians, astrologers, Chaldeans, and soothsayers" (5:11b), a catalogue that recalls for the reader as clearly as the queen's speech the former successes of the pagan court's Jewish wise man (1:20, 2:2,10,27; 4:7). Her phrases "master of the magicians," "in whom is the spirit of the holy gods," and "whom the king named Belteshazzar" (5:11,12) connect this narrative most closely with the fourth (4:8,9,18), suggesting that the story of Daniel's interpretation she remembers most vividly is the very one that Daniel will shortly rebuke Belshazzar with, the brutish humiliation of Nebuchadnezzar (5:20-21). "And thou his son, O Belshazzar, hast not humbled thine heart, *though thou knewest all this*" (5:22, italics added). Daniel's rebuke twice stresses Belshazzar's relationship with Nebuchadnezzar as son to father (5:18,22), echoing the stress in the queen's speech, in which she calls Nebuchadnezzar Belshazzar's father three times; Belshazzar himself refers to Nebuchadnezzar as "my father" (5:13).

This almost excessive repetition suggests that the author wishes to heighten the enormity of Belshazzar's failures as a king by portraying him as the son of the very man whose experiences should have taught Belshazzar how to judge wisely and how to avoid the pitfalls of his father by respecting and heeding Daniel and Daniel's God. Instead, though he states twice that he has "heard of" Daniel and his abilities (5:14,16), he obviously has never summoned Daniel to court or taken his wisdom seriously, and he has apparently forgotten until reminded in the present crisis that such a seer exists. From a literary point of view, the story, especially the feature of kingly relationships now under discussion, is tremendously effective. As I have postulated earlier, the author of Daniel deliberately includes historically erroneous and ahistorical elements to intensify his theme that the only reality is God and that the history, and the future, of human sovereignty is brief and illusory at best and nasty and brutish at worst. Thus learned discussions of Nebuchadnezzar, Belshazzar, Nabonidus, regencies, co-regencies, father meaning great grandfather, and so on, while valuable in their way are largely irrelevant to the literary, or the theological, power of this chapter or of this book.

six

The sixth and final narrative concerns the ruler who conquered Belshazzar, "Darius the Median," and the dramatic events which led to his recognizing, as Nebuchadnezzar had before him, the everlasting nature of the kingdom of Daniel's God (6:26-27), though the counterpart of that realization, that human kingdoms are ephemeral and subsumed always under the kingdom of God, never seems to have been fully recognized by any of the pagan monarchs in whose courts Daniel ministers. Divine deliverance has figured prominently in earlier narratives (the second and third especially), but in the sixth narrative God's ability and faithfulness to deliver those who trust him and obey him is the theme. Daniel's rapid rise to favor under Darius at the expense of other courtiers is reminiscent of his sudden preferment at the expense of others in former narratives (Chapters 1, 2, 4, and 5), but for the first time, his rise provokes retaliatory jealousy on the part of others (in this respect, as in others to be discussed below, the story has parallels with the third narrative in which Daniel's three friends are accused by enemies of not bowing to Nebuchadnezzar's image; however, no trap is laid). The "presidents and princes" seek some excuse for accusing Daniel of disobedience to the royal decrees, but his political conduct is so faultless that their efforts are vain (6:4).

Observing his steadfast devotion to the God and the Law of the Jews, his enemies devise a plan to catch Daniel in a dilemma between allegiance to his God or to his king, knowing that he will choose loyalty to God and his commands

(6:5). Darius, unperceptive of the jealous motives of his courtiers, accepts their advice that he

> establish a royal statute, and . . . make a firm decree, that whosoever shall ask a petition of any God or man for thirty days, save of [himself], he shall be cast into the den of lions.
>
> (Daniel 6:7b)

Daniel does not, of course, change his habitual practice of kneeling to pray while facing towards Jerusalem three times each day, and since "the law of the Medes and Persians . . . altered not" (6:8b), the king has unwittingly condemned Daniel to the lions and is powerless to deliver him. After a long night passes, during which Darius fasts, foregoes diversions, and cannot sleep because of concern for Daniel, sealed in the pit of lions, the morning finds the king "very early" at the site.

> He cried with a lamentable voice unto Daniel: . . .O Daniel, servant of the living God, is thy God, whom thou servest continually, able to deliver thee from the lions? Then said Daniel unto the king, O king, live forever. My God hath sent his angel, and hath shut the lions' mouths, and they have not hurt me.
>
> (Daniel 6:20-22)

The king rejoices in Daniel's deliverance, throws the malicious accusers—and their families!—to the lions, who chew them up, bones and all, before their bodies can touch the floor of the pit. Darius then decrees that all his subjects "tremble and fear before the God of Daniel [who] delivereth and rescueth, and . . . worketh signs and wonders in heaven and in earth" (6:26a,27a).

The similarities with the third narrative link the two stories, but there are significant differences as well; both the similarities and the differences serve to strengthen the impression of a deliberate effort to connect the third and sixth narratives. Shadrach, Meshach, and Abednego had just been elevated to powerful positions in Babylon before Nebuchadnezzar set up his image of gold; Daniel has just been made the first of three presidents over the kingdom and the king is considering giving him even more authority when a trap is laid for him (2:49-3:1; 6:1-3,5,6-9). In the earlier story, Nebuchadnezzar approaches the flaming furnace and calls out to the three friends because he has seen a fourth figure inside, which he later calls an ''angel''; Darius comes to the lions' den and calls out to Daniel to learn whether or not he has survived and Daniel reveals that an angel has protected him from the beasts (3:25-26; 6:20-21). Both Nebuchadnezzar and Darius respond to the supernatural deliverance of the Jews by issuing a decree protecting worshippers of the Hebrews' God and lauding him as a Deliverer *extraordinaire* (3:29; 6:26-27).

The differences parallel almost as neatly: Shadrach, Meshach, and Abednego's lives are threatened because of refusal to practice idolatry, whereas Daniel's is endangered because he refuses to cease praying—both are public acts of defiant loyalty to God (3:12,18; 6:10-11). Nebuchadnezzar reacts to the refusal in fury, but Darius blames himself and therefore seeks to deliver Daniel himself—that he does so without success underscores again how illusory human power is (3:13,19; 6:14). Those who throw the three friends into the flaming furnace are themselves killed in the effort, while Daniel's accusers are destroyed by the lions, and both turnabouts are the result of the monarch's command (3:20,22; 6:24). Nebuchadnezzar is sure no god can deliver the three friends from his fury, whereas Darius seems to believe, at least to hope, that God will rescue Daniel (3:15b; 6:16b,20b).

Building on such links as these similarities and differences and other links discussed earlier between other stories, scholars have proposed a system of concentric chiasmi for Chapters 2-7: 2 and 7 form the outside frame, 4 and 5 the center, and 3 and 6 the intermediate tier—see Figure 1 on page 46 (Lenglet, Casey, Raabe, Davies). Davies concludes that this chiastic structure is part of a design to draw the reader into ever closer contact with Daniel and then completely away from him at the end: in Chapters 1-6, Daniel is the object of narration, in 7-12 the reader subjectively identifies with Daniel as the speaker who addresses

the reader directly, and in the close of 12 Daniel is dismissed by the angel with
the words, "Go thy way, Daniel" (12:9) and the reader is dismissed by the angel
with a more general instruction, "Go thou thy way" (12:13; Davies). The
argument is attractive, but the reader may include himself without excluding
Daniel from the final words addressed to the blessed who wait with the hope of
standing at the end of the days. Since Daniel 2:4b through 7:28 is already unified
by the use of Aramaic, scholars have been encouraged to find other evidences of
a unified literary structure for Chapters 2-7; some argue for at least three authors
for the book: the first composed Chapters 2-7, the second wrote an introduction,
Chapter 1, in Hebrew, and a third (or a Danielic school of apocalyptic) wrote
Chapters 8-12 in Hebrew (e. g., Casey, Chapter 2).

Chapter 4

The Visions (Chapters 7-12)

The apocalyptic section of the Book of Daniel has been variously interpreted through the centuries. In what follows, I will provide an overview of the visions as I understand them after having read much of the scholarship, both of those committed, on the one hand, to the critical position that Daniel is a very late production intended to encourage Jews to resist the Hellenizing undertaken voluntarily by many Jews and mandated, ultimately with the use of force, by such rulers as Antiochus IV of Syria, and of those committed, on the other hand, to accepting the book at face value as a composition of the sixth century B. C., probably originally written by the prophet Daniel himself, and later edited by the Great Synagogue. The majority of serious Biblical scholars now believe that the Book of Daniel was actually composed in the second century B. C., that it is a pseudonymous work, and that it is an example of *vaticinium ex eventu*, "prophecy after the fact." Otto Eissfeldt, in his magisterial *The Old Testament: An Introduction*, dates Daniel between 167-163 B. C., but cites evidence which may even date the book as precisely as between December 164 and April 163!

Such a late dating is based on certain assumptions commonly held by modern Biblical scholars, among them that accurately predictive prophecy is always prophecy after the fact and that where a book contains historical errors the period in which historical events are described most accurately is bound to be the period of the book's origin (Eissfeldt 520-522; Towner 115). I have already discussed reasons why I do not believe the author of Daniel intends the first part of his book to be historically accurate, though I consider him to have been extremely careful about recording his prophetic visions and heavenly revelations as accurately as possible in the last half of his book. Some conservative scholars argue that the prophecies seen as after the fact by more liberal critics could be such, as in the example of identifying Antiochus IV as the "little horn" of Daniel 8, and, at the same time, such symbolic revelations "after the fact" could also be predictive of an "Anti-Christ" yet to be fulfilled beyond the future horizons of known history, as the New Testament writers appear to have believed (1 Thessalonians 2:3-4 with Daniel 11:36; Revelation 13:1-7 with Daniel 7:3-12, 21, 25).

One representative of this conservative view explains Daniel 11:29-45, for instance, as applying to Antiochus IV but not exclusively so, using the metaphor of "telescoping" prophecy, that is conflating past or present phenomena with future predictions, to indicate that the ultimate fulfillment of Daniel 11 may still be in the future, as the Apostle Paul apparently believed (Baldwin 199-203). It is perhaps best to conclude with Kvanvig that "It is possible to hold together both the historical context of the apocalypses [e. g., Daniel 7] and their relevance for later generations. The apocalypses . . . alluded to and reflected [, but] were not locked up in . . . concrete historical situations" (Kvanvig, "Relevance of Biblical Visions" 46).

Although the preceding discussion may appear to be designed to preface a theological interpretation of Daniel 7-12, it is not so intended. Neither by education, nor by extensive reading, nor by inclination am I prepared to indulge in doctrinaire interpretations of Daniel; any conclusions drawn here about meaning are based, to the best of my ability, on literary analyses, not theological ones.

one

Daniel's first vision (Chapter 7) is essentially a recapitulation of the substantive meaning of Nebuchadnezzar's dream in the second narrative (Chapter 2), but clothed in completely different and much more dynamically conceived imagery. For the head of gold, there is a lion with eagle's wings to represent Babylon; for the breast and arms of silver, there is a great bear with three ribs in its mouth to represent Medo-Persia; for the belly and thighs of brass (bronze), there is a winged leopard with four heads to represent the kingdom of Alexander the Great, ready to be subdivided into the kingdoms which followed his death.[14] For the legs of iron, there is a fourth indescribably dreadful beast with great iron teeth and ten horns to represent the arch-tyrant of Jewish history, Antiochus Epiphanes of Syria. At this point, as in the image of the ten toes of mingled iron and clay in Nebuchadnezzar's visionary image, known history (whether future or past from the writer of Daniel's point of view) is transcended; the significance of the "little horn" (7:8) who will war against the saints until destroyed by the Most High himself (7:9, 24-27), though probably referring to Antiochus most immediately, goes far beyond historical referent. For the stone that smashes Nebuchadnezzar's image and becomes a mountain filling the earth, there is the Ancient of Days, "one like the Son of Man" (7:13). When the Ancient of Days comes into the fray, he is seen in his chariot throne as Ezekiel saw him (7:9,10 with Ezekiel 1), and he brings to an end with phases of judgment and phases of dominion and destruction the ravages of the beasts (7:11-14). Understandably, the effort to comprehend, even to gaze at, such a vision causes Daniel physical pain as well as mental distress, and he asks an angelic bystander for help in understanding it (7:15-16). Without clarifying matters much beyond Daniel's narration of what he saw, the angel assures Daniel that the end of the matter will be like that seen in Nebuchadnezzar's dream: the kingdom of God will triumph over earthly kingdoms for the sake of the saints, and his kingdom will last forever (7:27 with 2:35,44).

This summary does not do justice to the vision's movement and color and violence and the anomalous character of the beasts; nor does it account for the traumatic impact of the vision on Daniel, though even the textual description hardly accounts for that. A reader must recall the narratives to appreciate fully how totally different Daniel's experience in Chapter 7 is from what precedes in the narratives. The vision of the great image in Nebuchadnezzar's dream is re-run for Daniel in answer to his and his friends' prayers, so he is an eye-witness to it (2:19); the statue is violently smashed by the stone "cut out without hands," but the images are relatively static except for that smashing and the wind which carries the broken pieces away. The huge tree in the dream of Chapter 4 is vividly described by Nebuchadnezzar and the description involves motion but only in anticipation; the heavenly watcher shouts his commands concerning the tree with striking verbs—hew, cut, shake, scatter, get away from under—but the actions are not carried out in the dream, and Daniel "sees" the scene only in his imagination as the king narrates it. His disturbed thoughts in the fourth narrative result not from the vision itself but from the rather delicate problem of bringing bad news to a respected but arbitrarily tyrannical monarch (4:19). In the fifth narrative, Daniel does not see the divine hand write on the wall, he sees only the completed writing, and though the message is one of destruction, Daniel seems to deliver it with some relish to the despicable Belshazzar. Finally in the sixth narrative, though Daniel faces real beasts in their lair, he is portrayed as calmly serene in contrast with the frenetically anxious Darius (6:19-22; cf. 6:14, 18).

The terrifying, surrealistic nightmare of Chapter 7, then, is a very different vision from anything that precedes it in the book; nothing has really prepared Daniel for such a shock. He is as troubled after the divine explanation as he was immediately after the vision (7:15,28). The conflict of four violent winds on the sea, the metamorphosis before his eyes of already incredible creatures into even more bizarre forms (a lion with a man's heart, a bear with ribs between its teeth distorted in its stance, a leopard with wings and four heads, an iron-toothed beast who sprouts a horn with human eyes and a mouth), the rapacious violence of the fourth beast, and the swiftly moving fiery throne of the Ancient of Days surrounded by millions of attendants—these are not scenes Daniel, or anyone for that matter, can view in calmly secure peace of mind.

Not only does the vision mark the watershed in the persona of Daniel in his book,[15] it so far exceeds the earlier visions and experiences of Daniel that the wonder is not that Daniel is so different in the last half of the book but that he can continue to function at all. That he does so is a tribute to his courage even in confusion and weakness; reflecting his purpose of heart to refuse the king's diet in Chapter 1, he stores this unfathomable mystery in his memory.

Two years later (these first two visions are flashbacks to the reign of Belshazzar, his first and third year respectively), things are no easier for Daniel; in fact, the strain becomes greater still. In the first vision, though it all was overwhelming, what concerned Daniel most was the fourth beast. His first request for "the truth of all this" (7:16) was answered very briefly; he presses for "the truth of the fourth beast" (7:19), and his second request, recounting his memory of the vision of the beast and his horn with eyes and a mouth (itself four times as lengthy as the angel's answer to his first question), indicates how obsessed above all else he is with that part of the vision (7:19-22). The explanation is elaborated on slightly, identifying the ten horns as ten kings, the "diverse" king (the little horn) as a persecutor of God's people who will ultimately be destroyed after flourishing in wickedness for "a time and times and the dividing of a time" (7:25), and assuring Daniel again that God and his saints will triumph (7:27).

two

Ironically Daniel notes at the end of Chapter 7: "Hitherto is the end of the matter" (7:28a), meaning "Here the explanation ends," but perhaps implying, "Enough already." But the fourth-beast vision is stored away in his heart and continues to trouble him, and Chapter 8 quickly makes clear that the matter is far from ended. The second vision expands in even more bizarre and frighteningly dynamic imagery the vision of the fourth beast of Chapter 7.[16] Alexander the Great is now a "he-goat [invading] from the west on the face of the whole earth," moving so swiftly that he does not touch the ground (8:5);[17] he destroys the Medo-Persian kingdom, figured forth by a ram with two horns. At the very zenith of his strength, the goat's horn is broken and in its place there spring up four horns (the four generals who, after Alexander's death, develop four kingdoms from his one, 8:8). Again the "little horn" is revealed as the arch-enemy of the "pleasant *land*" (literally, "the beauty," cf. 9:16,21); he desecrates the holy temple itself, and even casts down some of the stars of heaven (8:9-12). Once again Daniel is assured, this time by Gabriel (8:16), that this "little horn," who mysteriously fades into a supra-historical figure called "a king of fierce countenance" (8:23), will be destroyed, though only after he has destroyed many himself, by peace as well as by war (8:25): "he shall be broken without hand" (i.e., by Divine agency; cf. 2:34, the stone "cut out without hands"). As he had been deeply disturbed in mind and body by the vision of Chapter 7, Daniel is overcome mentally and physically; he faints and is in bed sick for days, and even after he is up and about court business again, his dismay and astonishment at what he has seen and heard continue.

Daniel's second vision affects him as deeply as his first, perhaps more so since when his heavenly instructor comes near he is afraid, falls into a trance prostrate on the ground, and has to be raised and encouraged by Gabriel, physical manifestations of trauma that are not associated with the first vision. Further, he is told to "shut . . . up the vision" (8:26) adding the strain of selective secrecy to the responsibility of reporting it. Daniel's curiosity about the fourth beast and the little horn, so unsatisfied by his interpreter in Chapter 7, is perhaps so fully gorged in Chapter 8, albeit with many features still like random pieces of a jigsaw puzzle that will almost but not quite fit together, that his turning in Chapter 9 to the prophetic scriptures may be as much to use them as a protective shield against more visions as to help him understand his visions. In any event, he is spared any more eye-witness experiences of horribly anomalous beasts fighting among themselves and against the saints. Gabriel appears again in his vision of Chapter 9 and in Chapter 10 he is overcome by a vision of "a certain man clothed in linen" (10:5) with characteristics very like the Ancient of Days (10:6 with 7:9), but though he again falls into a trance and must be tenderly raised and strengthened by his visitor, he sees no more frightening monsters. Instead his heavenly messenger uses narration to make him "understand what shall befall [his] people in the latter days" (10:14), finally instructing him to "shut up the words, and seal the book, *even* to the time of the end" (12:4,9).

three

Before being granted (or burdened with) more visions of any kind, then, Daniel enters into a relatively quiet period of study of Scripture and prayer. His reading of Jeremiah leads him to understand that the exile will last for seventy years because of Israel's sin in departing from God's holy covenant and neglecting the sabbaths of the Lord (9:2; Jeremiah 25:11, 29:10). Eloquently and with deep penitence for his people and for himself, he confesses and asks forgiveness for God's city and the people "called by [Yahweh's] name" (9:18,19). The angel Gabriel comes to explain that the number seventy has a significance for the future of Israel as well as for the present period of exile.

He prophesies to Daniel the decree of Cyrus by which the Jews can return to Jerusalem to restore and rebuild the city and the temple, and he reveals that from the time of that decree until Messiah comes will be sixty-nine weeks ("seven weeks, and threescore and two weeks," 9:25) of years, leaving one week of the "seventy weeks" of years yet to be fulfilled. The Messiah (literally, "anointed one") shall "be cut off, but not for himself" (9:26) and another destruction of the city and sanctuary will take place under the leadership of the mysterious "prince that shall come" (9:26). He will seem to make peace with the

Jews and respect their covenant for one week (seven years), but in the middle of that time (after three and one-half years) he will desecrate the temple and "cause the sacrifice and oblation to cease" (9:27). The events narrated by Gabriel are of the most serious nature for Daniel and his people and for the world, but the quiet narrative is a welcome relief for the reader as well as for Daniel after Chapters 7 and 8.

four

In Chapter 10, after a brief introduction referring to Daniel in the third person (the only place in the text between 7:2 and the end of the book that Daniel does not speak as first-person narrator), he relates his fourth and final vision and its exposition by a divine interpreter who helps him recover from the glorious appearance made to him by the river Hiddekel (the Tigris). Echoes of both Isaiah's and Ezekiel's experience pervade Chapter 10, even to Daniel's seeing himself as unclean (10:8 with Isaiah 6:5), falling dumb (10:5 with Ezekiel 3:26), and being raised from his prostrate position by his heavenly visitor (10:10-11 with Ezekiel 2:1-2). Chapters 11 and 12 are seen by most scholars as containing a fairly accurate description of the career and depredations of Antiochus IV: his struggles with Ptolemy of Egypt, and his persecutions of the Jews. Comparison with the account in the books of Maccabees will show how close the similarities are. The major discrepancy is the account of Antiochus' death in Chapter 11:40-45. "He shall plant the tabernacles of his palace [his royal tents] between the seas in the glorious holy mountain; yet he shall come to his end, and none shall help him" (11:45). We know from Polybius, however, that Antiochus died in Persia, not in Palestine (Jeffery 540; Hartman 305; 1 Maccabees 6:1-16).

The book closes with a promise of resurrection for both righteous and unrighteous (12:2), indications that the book is not intended to be clearly understood by those contemporaneous with its publication or for a long time afterward (12:4,9), mysterious and enormously intriguing references to numbers of days (12:11-12; cf. 8:14), and a quiet assurance to Daniel, and to all those who share his faith in the ultimate triumph of God and good, that rest and an appropriate standing in God's grace will be his, and theirs, "at the end of the days" (12:12), regardless of the number of days meant or the many events that must yet intervene. Figure 2 on page 46 represents graphically the thematic connections between narratives and visions.

Literary Influence

Within the Bible, the Book of Daniel is heavily influential on the imagery and style of the New Testament, most notably in the Book of Revelation and the Pauline epistles which touch on eschatology, but also in the Gospels and in the Book of Acts. John's opening vision of Christ in Revelation, for instance, is more indebted to Daniel than to any earlier scriptural author, though some phrases and images are borrowed as well from Zechariah, Isaiah, and Ezekiel (Revelation 1:7, 12-17, with Daniel 7:9,13; 10:5-6). John's visionary beasts from the sea and the earth, crowned and with horns, are monsters metamorphosed still more than Daniel's but still recognizable (Revelation 13 with Daniel 7), and the famous image of Michael and his angels warring in heaven against a dragon who casts down stars from heaven has a familiar ring to readers of Daniel (Revelation 12:3-4,7, with Daniel 7:3-6,7,25; 8:10; 10:13, 21; 12:1,7). One scholar counting citations to the Old Testament in Revelation finds "in terms of actual numbers of allusions" the following order: Isaiah, Ezekiel, Daniel, and Psalms. He points out, however, that an earlier commentator, H. B. Swete, had ranked the books alluded to in Revelation by number of allusions thus: Isaiah 46, Daniel 31, Ezekiel 29, Psalms 27 (Beale, "Revelation" 318). Whatever the numbers are, in terms of memorable images and communicating a sense of apocalyptic urgency, Daniel stands in the first rank of Hebrew prophets who influenced John's apocalypse.

The Book of Daniel's influence in English literature ranges from the Old English *Beowulf* to E. L. Doctorow's *The Book of Daniel* (Bosse, Müller). There is even an Old English poetic version of Daniel (Jost). Mark Mirsky comments, *a propos* of Milton's use of the angel Gabriel in *Paradise Lost*, "A writer in English who has been moved by Milton can not afford to ignore his sources in Daniel" (quoted in Rosenberg 449). The great British novelist George Eliot wrote, "The unknown teacher, to whom we are indebted for the Book of Daniel, is entitled to the praise that he was the first who grasped the history of the world, so far as he knew it, as one great whole, as a drama which moves onward at the will of the Eternal One" (Levine 27, quoted from the Pforzheimer MS., 710f [14]). Literary critics have praised the Book of Daniel as an inspiring example for developing striking imagery and giving organizational unity to diverse materials: the author employs a "style of literary painting [which has] a peculiar charm. . . .; [he has arranged] a series of separate scenes [drawn with] the strong strokes of frescoes, on the one side for the purposes of instruction by history, on the other for warning and encouragement by prophecy" (Preminger 292). Another critic writes, "Daniel has a style that is more closely reminiscent of oral epic than any other Old Testament narrative" (Ryken, *Literature of the Bible* 67). The same critic praises Chapters 1-6 of the Book of Daniel as "so thoroughly guided by the principle of heroic narrative that it violates a basic rule of narrative, unity of action" (Ryken, *Words of Delight* 109). Speaking of apocalyptic literature generally and of the Book of Revelation particularly, but in terms inclusive of Daniel, Northrop Frye describes the Apocalypse as

> primarily a vision of a body of imagery, where the images of every category of being—divine, angelic, paradisal, human, animal, vegetable and inorganic—are all identified with the body of Christ. Whatever is not part of the body of Christ forms a demonic shadow, a parody of the apocryphal vision in a context of evil and tyranny. This ultimate separation of vision from shadow, the heaven-world and the hell-world, is alluded to in the Gospel parables as a separation that human society cannot attain to in a world of time, but will see as the revelation that comes with the ending of time.
>
> (Frye, "Dialectic" 55-56)

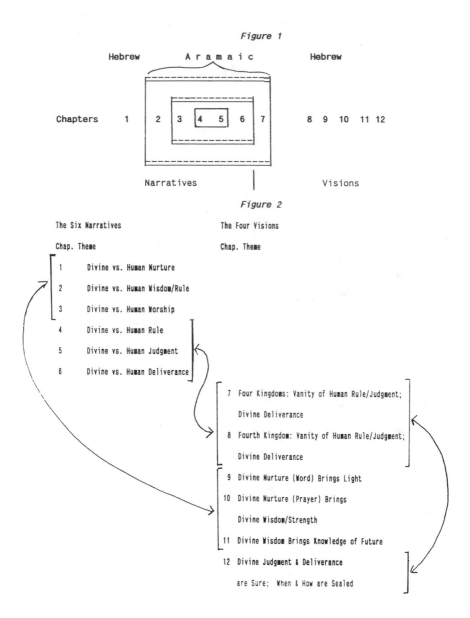

Figure 1

Hebrew   A r a m a i c   Hebrew

Chapters   1 | 2 3 |4 5| 6 7 | 8 9 10 11 12

Narratives | Visions

Figure 2

The Six Narratives   The Four Visions

Chap. Theme   Chap. Theme

1   Divine vs. Human Nurture

2   Divine vs. Human Wisdom/Rule

3   Divine vs. Human Worship

4   Divine vs. Human Rule

5   Divine vs. Human Judgment

6   Divine vs. Human Deliverance

7 Four Kingdoms: Vanity of Human Rule/Judgment;
   Divine Deliverance

8 Fourth Kingdom: Vanity of Human Rule/Judgment;
   Divine Deliverance

9 Divine Nurture (Word) Brings Light

10 Divine Nurture (Prayer) Brings
   Divine Wisdom/Strength

11 Divine Wisdom Brings Knowledge of Future

12 Divine Judgment & Deliverance
   are Sure; When & How are Sealed

Substitute Daniel's phrase "the saints of the Most High" for "the body of Christ" and "the Book of Daniel" for "the Gospel parables" and Frye's remarks aptly conclude a discussion of the Book of Daniel and point forward to the Apocalypse itself.

.

NOTES TO DANIEL

Some of the material in this essay appeared earlier in my "The Major Literary Prophecy of the Old Testament," *The Dalhousie Review*, 61 (1981): 447-468. A briefer version of this essay appears in *A Complete Literary Guide to the Bible*, eds. Leland Ryken and Tremper Longman III (Zondervan, 1993).

Scripture quotations, unless otherwise noted, are from the King James Version (NY: American Bible Society, 1967).

[1]See Yamauchi 458-466 for an extensive argument against Persian influence on Jewish apocalyptic. See also Millard 92 for evidence countering the view that nebrasta' in Dan. 5:5 is of Persian origin.

[2]Another view of the problem of Daniel's historicity is that of Slotki xiv. Noting that some historical details in the book cannot be reconciled with the ascertainable facts, he says, "It should be remembered that the 'ascertainable facts' increase with research and discovery. . . . who can say what will yet come to light?" One may not wish to subscribe unconditionally to Slotki's cautious dictum that "it is safest to accept the Biblical evidence as it is stated" in the realm of history, especially not when sound historical evidence contradicts it. The literary critic must certainly interpret a work as it lies before him and on its own terms. The *donné* must be accepted and the best (or the most) made of it.

In a personal letter to me, Ita Sheres suggests that "Daniel is not interested in the kings but rather in the priests and the ultimate outcome of the destruction in relation to the temple" and, therefore, is not concerned with historical accuracy. Furthermore, she writes, "the issue of historical error is moot for the apocalyptic visionary because the past as he sees it is of significance only [when placed] within a coherent present framework which [explains] to those who accept the vision what their role is and will be."

[3]Jewish translators of the Old Testament followed a standard technique, unique to them, of preserving the bilingual character of Daniel by translating the Hebrew portions in a language different from that used in translating the Aramaic passage. Altbauer 195 describes an example found in Codex 262 of the former Vilnius Public Library in Lithuania (now MS.F.19-262 of Library of the Academy of Sciences in Vilnius). Daniel 1:1-2:4a and 8-12 appear in the vernacular Belorussian of the early 16th century, while Daniel 2:4b-7:28 is "couched chiefly in the Slavonic used by Christian Orthodox Slavs in Muscovy and the Lithuanian Commonwealth."

[4]Grabbe 149-150 questions the consistency of religious faith in one who "writes an apologetic under the guise of scholarship," as he accuses fundamentalists of doing when they defend the historical accuracy of Daniel.

[5]In a special issue of *Semeia* devoted to consideration of stories in the Bible as comedy and/or tragedy, the Book of Daniel stimulated contrasting views on whether literary terms and methods are appropriate to Biblical material. Good 41-70 sees in Daniel 1-6 a structure similar to Old Comedy; Zakovitch 113 questions the appropriateness of measuring the Danielic narratives with a literary yardstick when their sequence is "the result of the (mistaken) historical construction of the book's editor." These essays are representative of the two extremes evident in many attempts of Bible critics and literary critics to pool their efforts. Good stretches the precise parts of Old Comedy too thin and wide to make

them fit the narratives of Daniel well, while Zakovitch relies on the standard scarecrow of the incompetent compiler/editor to shoo away efforts like Good's.

[6]Restating "the case for the unity of [Daniel]" (234), Rowley specifies the marks of unity as style, outlook, and "the community of error about Belshazzar and Darius the Mede" (272); he comments on the author's consistent quality of mind throughout as a "touch of looseness and inconcinnity" (272). Collins, *Daniel* 31, prefers to speak of "editorial unity" resulting from the book's two halves each including "a sequence of Babylonian, Median, and Persian rulers [reflecting] the scheme of Chs. 2 and 7, [the whole bound together by the] alternation of Hebrew and Aramaic." See also Stefanovic on "thematic links."

[7]Wills 144 postulates that Daniel 4, 5, and 6 may have "circulated together before being combined first with chapters 1-3 and then with 7-12 and the additions [The Prayer of Azariah, The Song of the Young Men, Susanna, and Bel and the Dragon]" and argues for placing both Daniel 1-6 and Esther in the genre of wisdom court legend. G. H. Wilson 374 argues against connecting Daniel with wisdom literature because certain words characteristic of wisdom books like Job and Ecclesiastes, though used in Daniel, are *not* used as key words for their "inherent value" but are used in appropriately literary ways.

[8]It is surprising, given the way the Daniel narratives communicate their message so effectively through their mutual juxtaposition as well as through the individual accounts, that Meir Sternberg, in demonstrating that "the Bible's forte is the art of context" (458) refers to Daniel only four times and never considers the narrative art of Daniel. Daniel 1-6 could profitably have been included in Sternberg's fine chapter on "The Structure of Repetition: Strategies of Informational Redundancy."

[9]Talmon 347-348 cites Daniel and his three companions as one example among many others of the "ascending numerical pattern 3 + 1, observable in other Near-Eastern literatures," and reflected in the stories of Balaam, Job, and David, as well as in the structure of parts of Proverbs.

[10]Collins 230 refers to the Prayer of Nabonidus from Qumran (4QPrNab) as part of a tradition that Daniel draws on for the content of Chapter 4.

[11]The Hebrew version of Daniel treats 4:1-3 as the conclusion of the third narrative, or 3:31-33. The content is clearly relevant to both chapters. Perhaps the passage should be seen as both a conclusion to the third narrative and a prologue to the fourth.

[12]Openshaw 171 discusses an eleventh-century cycle of illustrations of the Book of Daniel in the Roda Bible (Paris BN Lat.6, four volumes), the longest Daniel cycle to survive the Middle Ages. One of the most striking groups of illustrations is that representing the fourth narrative. The huge tree is filled with fruit, leaves, and birds, and under its spreading branches are many animals, some of which anticipate the beasts of Daniel 7-8. God and the watcher are represented by a human hand pointing down the trunk toward the tree's base, where axemen stand on either side with axes poised to strike. Two lower registers show Daniel interpreting the dream to the king, flanked by a group of wise men in consternation, and Nebuchadnezzar on all fours among beasts, naked, with long hair and nails. This Daniel cycle is longer than that for any other book in the Roda Bible, and the illustrations of Daniel outnumber by two to one those in any other extant Medieval Bible. Openshaw explains the greater interest in Daniel in Spain than elsewhere in the period as reflecting Spanish hopes for the overthrow of "idolatrous" Moors, since the reconquest of Spain from the Moslems had been recognized as a crusade by the papacy.

[13]Northrop Frye, discussing the images of Leviathan and Behemoth in Job, describes Nebuchadnezzar's beastly form as "a variety of the behemoth . . . parallel to Ezekiel's earlier identification of the leviathan with the Pharaoh of Egypt" (Frye, Great Code 191).

[14]Only two of the generals who divided Alexander's kingdom among themselves after his death concern the history of the Jews. Seleucus I gained control of Babylon, Persia, and Syria; Ptolemy seized Egypt. Thus Israel (more

properly, Judah) was caught between two powerful kings struggling to control the trade routes that criss-crossed Palestine and to gain undisputed access to the eastern end of the Mediterranean.

[15]That Chapter 7 "forms a bridge between" 1-6 and 8-12 (Collins, *Apocalyptic Imagination)* is noted by many scholars, using various metaphors. For example, Lacoque 13 refers to the chapter as a "transition entre les deux genres et participant des deux"; Raabe 267 calls it "a hinge which binds together chapters 1-6 and 8-12"; Porteous 95 sees it as "the heart of the Book . . . related so closely to what precedes and . . . what follows" that it is difficult to decide whether to link it "more closely with the former or . . . the latter." I suggest here that it is also the literary turning point *(agnorisis, peripiteia,* or both) for the character of Daniel.

[16]Porter xi examines fully sources for and analogues to the anomalous beasts of Chapters 7 and 8. Briefly stated, his thesis is that "Daniel's animal metaphors in their complexity find their roots in the OT and ancient near Eastern notions of the shepherd king."

[17]Steiner 130, reviewing Peter Green's biography of Alexander, describes Alexander's swift troop movements in language that calls vividly to mind Daniel's image of the "he goat [which] came from the west on the face of the whole earth, and touched not the ground" (8:5). In an early campaign, his army marched "two hundred and fifty miles in less than a fortnight, . . . eighteen and twenty miles a day under full armament. . . . In the thrust toward the Caspian [Alexander's army] averaged thirty-six miles daily over terrain that defies modern transport. . . . Only Napoleon, only Rommel and Patton (and they were motorized) have matched the speed, the successive hammer blows, the genius of surprise in Alexander's campaigns."

WORKS CITED FOR DANIEL

Altbauer, M. "Contacts between Christians and Jews in the Field of Bible Translation." *Harvard Ukranian Studies* (1988-89): 194-199.

Alter, Robert, and Frank Kermode, eds. *The Literary Guide to the Bible.* Cambridge, MA: Belknap P of Harvard UP, 1987.

Baldwin, J. G. *Daniel: An Introduction and Commentary.* Urbana: InterVarsity P, 1978.

Beale, G. K. *The Use of Daniel in Jewish Apocalyptic Literature and in the Revelation of St. John.* Lanham, MD: UP of America, 1984.

_____. "Revelation." *It is Written: Scripture Citing Scripture. Essays in Honour of Barnabas Lindars.* Eds. D. A. Carson and H. G. M. Williamson. Cambridge: Cambridge UP, 1988. 318-336.

Birch, Bruce C. "What Does the Lord Require (Part 6)?: Sages, Visionaries, and Poets—Pluralism in Post-Exilic Israel." *Sojourners*, 13 (1984): 25-28.

Bosse, Roberta Bux and Jennifer Lee Wyatt. "Hrothgar and Nebuchadnezzar: Conversion in Old English Verse." *Papers on Language and Literature,* 23 (Summer 1987): 3, 257-271.

Burkholder, Byron. "Literary Patterns and God's Sovereignty in Daniel 4." *Direction*, 16 (Fall 1987): 45-54.

Casey, Maurice. *Son of Man: The Interpretation and Influence of Daniel 7.*
    London: Society for the Promotion of Christian Knowledge, 1979.

Collins, John J. *The Apocalyptic Imagination: An Introduction to the Jewish
    Matrix of Christianity.* New York: Crossroad, 1984.

_____. *Daniel. With An Introduction to Apocalyptic Literature.* Grand Rapids: W.
    B. Eerdmans, 1984.

Davies, Philip R. *Daniel.* Sheffield: Journal for the Study of the Old Testament
    P, 1988.

Eissfeldt, Otto. *The Old Testament: An Introduction.* Trans. Peter A. Ackroyd.
    New York: Harper and Row, 1965.

Fewell, Danna Nolan. *Circle of Sovereignty: A Story of Stories in Daniel 1-6.*
    Sheffield: The Almond P, 1988.

Frye, Northrop. "The Dialectic of Belief and Vision." *Shenandoah*, 39 (Fall
    1989), 3: 47-64.

_____. *The Great Code: The Bible and Literature.* New York: Harcourt Brace
    Jovanovich, 1982.

Good, Edwin M. "Apocalyptic as Comedy: The Book of Daniel." *Semeia*, 32
    (1984): 41-70.

Grabbe, Lester L. "Fundamentalism and Scholarship: The Case of Daniel."
    *Scripture: Meaning and Method: Essays Presented to Anthony Tyrrell
    Hanson.* Ed. Barry P. Thomson. Hull: Hull UP, 1987.

Gunn, David M. "The Anatomy of Divine Comedy: On Reading the Bible as
    Comedy and Tragedy." *Semeia*, 32 (1984): 115-129.

Hartman, Louis F. and Alexander A. DiLella, eds. *The Book of Daniel.* The
    Anchor Bible, Vol. 23. Garden City: Doubleday and Co., 1978.

Jeffery, Arthur. "Introduction and Exegesis to Daniel." George Arthur Buttrick,
    et al., eds. *The Interpreters Bible,* Vol. VI. New York & Nashville:
    Abingdon P, 1956.

Jost, David A. "Biblical Sources of Old English Daniel." *English Language Notes,* 15: 257-263.

Kvanvig, Helge S. "The Relevance of the Biblical Visions of the End-Time: Hermeneutical Guidelines to the Apocalyptical Literature." *Horizons in Biblical Theology,* 11 (1989): 35-58.

_____. *Roots of Apocalyptic: The Mesopotamian Background of the Enoch Figure and of the Son of Man. Wissenschaftliche Monographien zum Alten und Neuen Testament.* Meubinchenvluyn: Neukirchener Verlag, 1988.

Lacocque, André. *Le Livre de Daniel. Commentaire de L'Ancien Testament, XVb.* Paris: Delachaux et Niestle, Editeurs Neuchatel, 1976. Trans. David Pellauer as *The Book of Daniel.* Atlanta: John Knox P, 1979.

Lasine, Stuart. "Solomon, Daniel, and the Detective Story: The Social Functions of a Literary Genre." *Hebrew Annual Review,* 11 (1987): 247-266.

Lenglet, P. "La Structure littéraire de Daniel 2-7." *Biblica,* 53 (1972): 172-190.

Levine, George. "George Eliot's Hypothesis of Reality (Derived from Daniel)." *Nineteenth-Century Fiction,* 35 (1990): 1-28.

Millard, A. R. "The Etymology of nebrasta', Daniel 5:5." *Maarv,* 4 (Spring 1987), 1:87-92.

Müller, Kurt. "Biblische Typologie im zeitgenossischen judischamerikanischen Roman: E. L. Doctorow's *The Book of Daniel* and Bernard Malamud's *God's Grace." Paradeigmata: Literarische Typologie des Alten Testament,* II:20. Ed. Franz Link. Berlin: Duncker & Humlot, 1989.

NEB: *The New English Bible with the Apocrypha: Oxford Study Edition.* Gen. Ed. Samuel Sandmel. New York: Oxford UP, 1976.

Newsome, James D., Jr. *The Hebrew Prophets.* Atlanta: John Knox P, 1984.

NRSV: *The New Oxford Annotated Bible with the Apocryphal/Deuterocanonical Books.* Eds. Bruce M. Metzger and Roland E. Murphy. New York: Oxford UP, 1991.

Openshaw, Kathleen M. "The Daniel Cycle in the Roda Bible: An Expression of Its Age." *Proceedings and Transactions of the Royal Society of Canada,* 23 (1985): 158-172.

Porteous, Norman W. *Daniel: A Commentary.* Philadelphia: Westminster P, 1965.

Porter, Paul A. *Metaphors and Monsters: A Literary-Critical Study of Daniel 7 and 8.* Coneictanea Biblica, OT Series 20. Uppsala: CWK Gleerup, 1983.

Preminger, Alex and Edward L. Greenstein. *The Hebrew Bible in Literary Criticism.* New York: Ungar Publishing Co., 1986.

Raabe, Paul R. "Daniel 7: Its Structure and Role in the Book." *Biblical and Other Studies in Memory of S. D. Goitein.* Ed. Reuben Ahroni. *Hebrew Annual Review,* 9 (1985): 267-275.

Rosenberg, David, ed. *Congregation: Contemporary Writers Read the Jewish Bible.* San Diego: Harcourt Brace Jovanovich, 1987.

Rowland, Christopher. "Apocalyptic Literature." *It is Written: Scripture Citing Scripture.* Eds. D. A. Carson and H. G. M. Williamson. Cambridge: Cambridge UP, 1988. 170-189.

Rowley, H. H. *The Relevance of Apocalyptic.* London: Lutterworth P, 1944.

_____. "The Unity of the Book of Daniel." *Hebrew Union College Annual,* 23, Pt. 1 (1951): 233-273.

Ryken, Leland. *The Literature of the Bible.* Grand Rapids: Zondervan Publishing House, 1974.

_____. *Words of Delight: A Literary Introduction to the Bible.* Grand Rapids: Baker Book House, 1987.

Sandmel, Samuel. *The Hebrew Scriptures: An Introduction to Their Literature and Religious Ideas.* New York: Alfred A. Knopf, 1963.

Sims, James H. *The Bible in Milton's Epics.* Gainesville: University of Florida P, 1962.

Slotki, J. J., ed. *Daniel.* The Soncino Bible. London: Soncino P, 1950.

Stefanovic, Zdravko. "Thematic Links Between the Historical and Prophetic Sections of Daniel." *Andrews University Seminary Studies*, 27 (Summer 1989): 121-127.

Steiner, George. "Golden Boy." Review of Peter Green, *Alexander of Macedon, 356-323 B. C. The New Yorker*, Dec. 9, 1991: 129-131.

Sternberg, Meir. *The Poetics of Biblical Narrative: Ideological Literature and the Drama of Reading*. Bloomington: Indiana UP, 1987.

Talmon, Shemaryahu. "Daniel." *The Literary Guide to the Bible*. Eds. Robert Alter and Frank Kermode. Cambridge: Belknap P of Harvard UP, 1987. 343-356.

Towner, W. Sibley. *Daniel*. Atlanta: John Knox P, 1984.

Wills, Lawrence M. *The Jew in the Court of the Foreign King: Ancient Jewish Court Legends*. Harvard Dissertations in Religion, 26. Minneapolis: Fortress P, 1990.

Wilson, Gerald H. "Wisdom in Daniel and the Origin of Apocalyptic." *Hebrew Annual Review*, 9 (1985): 373-381.

Wilson, Robert R. "From Prophecy to Apocalyptic: Reflections on the Shape of Israelite Religion." *Semeia*, 21 (1981): 79-95.

Yamauchi, Edwin M. *Persia and the Bible*. Grand Rapids: Baker Book House, 1990.

Zakovitch, Yair. "U and Ո in the Bible." *Semeia*, 32 (1984), 107-114. (A response to Good.)

PART II
THE BOOK OF REVELATION

Behold, the tabernacle of God is with men,
and he will dwell with them,
and they shall be his people,
and God himself shall be with them.
(Revelation 21:3)

Introduction

Even a cursory survey of the vast landscape of critical and interpretive writing on Revelation is likely to make one weep with John "because no man [has been] found worthy to open" its mysteries to the clear understanding of the reader (Rev. 5:4). The grief and frustration of the apostle was greatly relieved by the opening of the seals and the visions consequent to that opening, though what was revealed to him occasioned renewed grief for mankind and the world as well as joy in the triumph of God's righteousness through the risen Christ. But many readers of Revelation—at once aware of the divine blessing promised those who read and observe the counsel of John's book (Rev. 1:3; 22:7), the divine curse pronounced on those who add to or subtract from the book's contents (Rev. 22:18-19), the divine prohibition preventing his including in the book some of the heavenly counsel made known to him (Rev. 10:4), *and* the final divine command to John to "seal not" the prophetic content because of the imminence of the time of the end (Rev. 22:10)—may find their confusion confounded by the very visions which remove John's fears and lead him to welcome the swift fulfillment of those visions in the Lord's coming (Rev. 22:20). For such readers, sensitive already to Revelation's apparent contradictions, there is little wonder that scholarly (and preacherly) commentary and criticism tend rather to add to the confusion than to dissipate it, and while they can hardly be blamed for pronouncing a pox on both the text and its would-be explicators and vowing to read no further, my plea to such readers is to continue seeking to receive the blessing promised to persevering students of Revelation. My efforts, and those of others, may succeed only in that they drive readers continually back to the text to find that the greatest rewards may lie in the search itself rather than in discovery of the searched-for. As Susan Schneiders has persuasively argued, the biblical text, the "revelatory text," functions "as locus and mediator of transformative encounter with the living God" only when it is actively engaged on its own terms, that is as sacred scripture (197). Elisabeth Schüssler Fiorenza, in a similar comment, insists "that the meaning of Rev[elation] cannot be found behind the text but is given with the text and its rhetorical function" *(Justice* 26).[1] My intention, too, is to focus on the text as it has come down to us and to seek for its meaning in a literary analysis of the book in concert with a similar analysis of the Book of Daniel. I do not, as Fiorenza does, seek to relate the rhetoric of Revelation to a rhetorical situation within the socio-political context contemporary with the book's composition. I do, however, heed her warning, given in another context, that a "formalistic literary understanding of Revelation [may overlook] the fact that John did not write art for art's sake, but that he had a definite purpose in mind" ("Revelation" 418). This study is an attempt to understand Revelation better by analyzing it in the context of the preceding analysis of the Book of Daniel. Unsolved mysteries remain in both books, but it is my hope that a similar approach to the two books in tandem yields sufficient enlightenment to justify the reader's time in reading as well as my own time in having written this work. As I began work on Daniel and Revelation, I was surprised to find only a few book-length works which deal jointly with these two biblical books: Rushdoony, *Thy Kingdom Come* (1971); Efird, *Daniel and Revelation* (1978); Michelson, *Daniel and Revelation* (1984); and Beale, *The Use of Daniel in Jewish Apocalyptic Literature and in the Revelation of St. John* (1984).

In fact only the latter seeks to interrelate the two texts instead of simply including discrete studies of each book within the same binding. Beale, therefore, has been by far the most helpful, demonstrating as he does that while John was acquainted with both Christian and Jewish apocalyptic traditions based on Daniel, the "Danielic parallels which Revelation has in common with Jewish apocalyptic are directly related to ideas about Christ's death, resurrection, present reign and future coming," not with the peculiarly Jewish hopes which concern Jewish pocalyptists (328). Beale's study of John's use of Daniel in Revelation leads him to conclude the probability that the apocalyptic chapters of Daniel provide "the most formative influence on the thought and structure of Revelation" (297). My own study, however, convinces me that the narrative section of Daniel is also important in shaping the form and suggesting some of the content of Revelation.

A perennial problem in criticism of Revelation is the question of whether or not the author may be identified with the author of the Gospel and the Epistles of John; a helpful summary of critical schools of thought on the question is provided in Fiorenza (*Justice* 85-113). While my study will not directly address this issue, my own mental bent, despite some conflicting evidence, is to give considerable weight to the connections—allusive thought patterns, theological links, some common language usage, structural similarities, and an assumed "audience of similar character"—persuasively argued by Smalley (553, 555, 559-560, 563-566), and thus to consider the John of Revelation the same writer as the John of the Fourth Gospel.

Of more interest in this study than authorial identity, however, are the similarities between the figure of the hero/narrator/prophet in Revelation and the central character in Daniel. Both Daniel and John must endure the status of religious and political enemy of the state, one as captive slave, the other as exile; both are known by names highly respected in other biblical texts, Daniel in Ezekiel and the Apocrypha and John in the gospels and the epistles; both use dense systems of symbolic imagery to interpret God's actions as they relate to his beloved people in the past, the present, and the future; both are essentially lone figures seeking to communicate Heaven's messages to human communities from whose immediate fellowship they are cut off (Daniel's three friends disappear early in his book); and both are frail men of flesh who must be strengthened and upheld by supernatural characters in order to carry out their prophetic missions. Both play roles which vary from first-person narration to third-person participation in narrated action, and in each case the generic mode of writing is mixed:

narrative combined with prophetic utterance and apocalyptic vision in Daniel, epistolary framework encompassing prophetic utterance and apocalyptic vision in Revelation. Finally both are self-conscious authors concerned deeply about textual authority and feeling the burden of faithfully recording (or concealing on occasion) the visions granted them by heaven. One could say of both Daniel and John what one scholar has said of John alone: "in many ways [his book is] a book about books" (Payne 366). And Martin Buber has in mind both authors when he says, "The apocalyptic writer has no audience turned toward him; he speaks into his notebook. He does not really speak, he only writes; he does not write down his speech, he just writes his thoughts—he writes a book" (180).

Revelation follows the pattern of Daniel in the distancing of the prophet from God by means of intermediaries. Such distancing is not a factor in the narrative section of Daniel since he is a third-person character in stories told about him by an effaced, omniscient narrator. When the major apocryphal visions begin, however, the pattern is set: the Ancient of Days mediates through the Son of man and a bystander ("one of them who stood by," an angel) the message Daniel is to gather from the dream of the four beasts (Dan. 7:13-16); that is, Daniel's stance is characteristically at a third remove from God. Similarly, Revelation, which launches immediately into apocalyptic form by using the word itself, places John at a third remove from God: God gives the revelation, literally the apocalypse, to Jesus Christ, who in turn transmits the message through an angel to John (Rev. 1:1).[2] This pattern continues throughout both books: in Daniel, the intermediaries between God and Daniel vary, but there are always at least two (Dan. 8:15-17, a "man" and Gabriel; 9:2-3,19-23, the Scriptures and Gabriel; 10:12-14,21, the Scriptures and an angel, apparently Gabriel). In Revelation John is similarly placed (Rev. 5:1-5, an angel and an elder; 10:1-11, an angel with a book and a "voice"; 21:9-10, a "great voice" and one of the seven angels with vials of plagues). The single exception, all the more striking for its departure from the pattern of Daniel and Revelation both, occurs when "he that sat upon the throne," identified by the context as God himself, speaks directly to John: "Write: for these words are true and faithful . . . . It is done" (Rev. 21:5-6 in the context of 21:1-8). Appropriately, as heaven and earth are seen united under God's sovereign rule, the intermediaries between human messenger and God are removed for a moment. It is as though Christ's promise that overcomers will be on his throne as he is on his Father's (3:21) is fulfilled and John, representative of redeemed mankind, the Son, and God himself have joined in one throne (cf. 1 Cor. 15:24-28).[3] Then, since this universal union is "not yet," the remainder of the vision is mediated by an angel, a "fellow servant," speaking for Jesus Christ (22:6-9).

The central message transmitted through the similar figure of a distanced human prophet by means of diverse literary forms in both apocalypses is the same: God's divine sovereignty is certain to bring ultimate victory to God's people who are suffering evil days under demonic earthly rulers. This happy ending will occur at an undisclosed future "time of the end" in Daniel and at a time unknown but very near ("things which must shortly come to pass") and therefore to be continuously expected in Revelation.

Chapter 5

Genre, Date, and Principles of Interpretation

The mixed nature of Revelation's form is evident from the first chapter. The first noun is "Revelation" ("Apocalypse," from Greek *apokalyptein*, "to disclose the hidden"), an explicit connection with the apocalyptic tradition and a declaration of genre. Yet this book is not, despite the irony of its traditional editorial title, the "Apocalypse of St. John"; it is the "Apocalypse of Jesus Christ," given to Jesus by God and in turn communicated to the servants of Jesus by means of one of those servants, namely John (Rev. 1:1). Thus having named the book not just another apocalypse but *the* apocalypse of God himself, the author immediately associates the book with the prophetic tradition by use of the formula "his servant John, who bare record of the word of God" and the designation of his book as "this prophecy" (Rev. 1:2-3; cf., e.g., Jer. 1:4, Ezek. 1:3, Hos. 1:2, Joel 1:1, Amos 7:15). Next, without transition, he uses the literary form of the pastoral letter so familiar to Christians from the epistles of Paul, a pattern found in letters preserved in Greek papyri (Pritchard 216; John White 9-11): greeting with signature, identification of addressee(s), expression of good wishes, prayer of thanks to the deity, message.[4] Finally he combines apocalyptic and epistolary devices in the remainder of Chapter 1 (9-20) as an introduction to the letters to the seven churches (Chapters 2-3), each of which repeats apocalyptic features from the first chapter and foreshadows apocalyptic symbols from the end of the book while predicting, as in prophecy, blessings and curses to follow certain kinds of obedient or disobedient behavior (e.g., Rev. 2:1 with 1:12,13; 2:7 with 22:2; 22:5; cf. the Mosaic prophecy of Deut. 28:58-59, 30:9-10). The book's close is itself epistolary in form, yet with aspects of both apocalypse and prophecy intertwined (Rev. 22:18-21 with 1-5, 6-10, 11-17).

Of the various forms used in the composition of the Book of Revelation the most predominant is the apocalyptic, though the prominent epistolary features which frame the whole may have played an important part in the book's finally unquestioned status within the canon of the New Testament (in the Western tradition at least),[5] perhaps through association with the apostolic letters attributed to Paul. Indeed Revelation and the epistles of Paul may have served in the first century to help authenticate each other through their similarities in form as well as their likenesses in eschatological emphases and their first-person relation of ecstatic visionary experiences. Fiorenza, bothered by scholars' reluctance to classify Revelation with early Christian prophecy, has developed a convincing model of interpretation that can accommodate Revelation within the context of "early Christian prophecy in Asia Minor at the end of the first century C.E."(*Justice* 134, 146-152). And as Buber says in "Prophecy, Apocalyptic, and the Historical Hour": "[W]herever a living historical dialogue of divine and human actions breaks through there persists, visible or invisible, a bond with the prophecy of Israel" (183).

Revelation, then, while it has roots in both Jewish and Christian apocalyptic tradition and deserves to be regarded primarily as an apocalypse, should no longer be categorized as narrowly as this; its amalgamation of apocalyptic and epistolary features and its alignment with the prophetic tradition in both testaments mark it as a distinctive literary achievement and add to one's sense of the appropriateness with which the book holds its position as a conclusion to the entire canon of Christian Scripture.

Date

Suggested dates for Revelation range from as early as A. D. 64-70, based on internal evidence linking Chapters 11, 17, and 18 with historical events in Jerusalem and Rome just prior to the destruction of the Temple (Robinson, Bell), or A. D. 68-69, based on the argument that "L'Apocalypse est . . . une oeuvre juive in l'origine [et] reflète . . . la guerre anti-romaine [et anti-Néron] de Judée de 63-70" (Bodinger 34); through A. D. 95 under the Emperor Domitian, well after the Temple's destruction (Hemer, Freyne); to as late as A. D. 110-114, based on a comparison of the letters of Revelation and those of Ignatius, letters that all seem to reflect the same struggles in the church against groups holding views considered heretical (Kraft). Fiorenza favors as "most promising [a date] within the context of early Christian development" ("Revelation" 414).[6] Freyne, however, focusing on the "little apocalypse" in Hebrews 12:22-24; 13:14, and comparing it with Revelation 21:9-27, comments that both books "would appear to have the actual post-[A.D.] 70 situation in view when a restructuring of the symbolic world that the temple [had] represented was called for" (93). Probably the middle ground of the debate, *circa* A. D. 95-100, is slightly more defensible than the very early or much later dates. The major alternatives and their attendant problems are summarized by Collins ("Dating" 33-45).

Principles of Interpretation

Revelation has been read in multifarious ways, but most of those ways could be grouped under two large headings: historical and eschatological. John M. Court (Chapter 1) details eight types of exegesis in interpreting Revelation: chiliastic (i.e., focused on a millennial reign of Christ), allegorical, recapitulative, historical-prophetic, eschatological, historical-contemporary, literary, and comparative. As McGinn points out, these "modes of exegesis are not discrete entities, but usually intermingle" in the interpretation given by individual scholars (23).

Historical interpretations include those which see Revelation as interpreting past history, prophesying future events, interpreting history contemporary with the author, or some combination of these into specialized "histories": salvation history, history of the church, theology/philosophy of history. Any of these historical approaches may emphasize allegory, literary technique, comparative apocalyptics, linear or cyclical presentation, or millennialism. Similarly the emphasis in eschatological interpretations may be on any of these exegetical modes. What separates historical from eschatological interpretation, then, is not the analytical procedure of the interpreter; it is the thematic orientation of the interpreter which in turn determines toward what kind of results he will direct his exegesis.

Using an apt metaphor for this thematic orientation, Fiorenza argues that eschatology is the "proper horizon for the understanding of Revelation" *(Justice* 46). In other words, John's aim is not to legitimate apocalyptic eschatology by a certain course of historical events, whether past, present, or future; neither is he concerned with the significance of world history as a determiner of how the end will unfold. His main concern is to encourage and strengthen the Christian community by showing that history is subordinate to God's kingdom which can break in to history at any moment, destroying godless powers, judging both dead and living, and joining heaven and earth in a happy union like that enjoyed in the Garden of Eden. In Fiorenza's words, the author of Revelation "does not seek to comfort the persecuted Christian community with reference to past and future history, but with reference to the eschatological reality of God's kingdom. This main theme of Rev[elation] is shortly but precisely expressed in the hymn in 11:16-19 which is composed in the center of the book" (*Justice* 56).[7]

The entire content of visions and images in Revelation, then, is determined by the imminent expectation of that appearance of Christ "which must shortly come to pass" and is the content of "The Revelation of Jesus Christ" (1:1). To use eschatology as the "proper horizon," however, is not to omit consideration of history—past, present, future—but to subjugate it to eschatology, rather than the other way round. The "short time" and the anticipation of reality's bursting into mankind's vanity fair forces one's perspective toward the triumph of God and good in the world even as it intensifies, through John's visions, the pain, persecution, and even martyrdom that must precede the happy resolution of all earthly problems stemming from the Fall in Genesis (Rev. 6:11, 22:1-3; Gen. 2:8-9, 3:22-24).

John in Revelation, as does Daniel in his book before John, stresses both the "already" and the "not yet" of God's rule in the kingdom of men, but in John the emphasis falls more on the latter with an important addition: "not yet, but *soon*." Perhaps the most significant similarity between Daniel and John's Revelation is the recurring theme that the sovereign Lord God is in control both in heaven and in earth; therefore, whether one's view is fixed on the "already" or the "not yet," on history or on eschatology—or on both—one must also exercise a transcendent vision that recognizes that the true locus of "everlasting dominion," of a "reign [to last] for ever and ever," is in God (Dan. 7:13, Rev. 22:5), not in man nor in man's deeds.

Chapter 6

Literary Analysis: The Book as a Whole

Revelation consists of a prologue (Chapter 1), an epistolary section devoted to messages to the seven churches of Asia Minor (Chapters 2-3), a series of apocalyptic visions and narration closing with divine judgment of the dead (Chapters 4-20), a triumphant apocalyptic vision of a renewed beneficent heaven and an edenic earth reunited under God and his Son who rule in sovereignty from the holy city, New Jerusalem (Chapter 21:1-22:5), and an epilogue (22:6-21).

Before moving to a closer literary look at each section here outlined, in order to help the reader grasp and perhaps hold in mind an overview of the whole, I shall briefly summarize the features of each section, features which show the Apocalypse to be an artistically crafted and a thematically unified and engaging work. Leonard L. Thompson, in ''The Literary Unity of the Book of Revelation,'' has masterfully suggested the richness and variety of John's artistry; he explores ''some of the ways. . .the seer has unified his work'' (347): contrasting units, equivalence of measure, reversed relationships, image accumulation, concentric developments, clustering of figures, irony, puns, and mythic patterns. Thompson's essay is a daring demonstration of the unbroken wholeness of Revelation made up of many disparate parts, and all that he describes is there and God's plenty besides. My own effort, however, is to reveal how larger parts also interrelate to create wholeness and, finally, to suggest some of the similarities and differences between John's dazzling literary architecture and Daniel's much earlier but equally skillful crafting of apocalyptic narrative and prophecy. After all, we must remind ourselves, John had in Daniel a clearer and more unified literary antecedent both to echo and purposefully veer from than Daniel ever had.

Prologue and Epilogue (1:1-20, 22:6-21)

The prologue and the epilogue are carefully designed as corresponding frames for the book as a whole: God's purpose in the book is to show his will to his servants (1:1 with 22:6), and to pronounce a special blessing on readers and observers of the book's content (1:3 with 22:7); John identifies himself as the messenger through whom the visionary messages are revealed (1:9 with 22:8) and falls down before the divine presence—in the prologue overwhelmed by the appearance of the Son of man, in the epilogue seeking instinctively but incorrectly to worship an angel (1:17 with 22:8); Jesus proclaims himself the Alpha and the Omega (1:8,11 with 22:13) and stresses that what he reveals will "shortly" come to pass, for he will "come quickly" (1:1,3 with 22:6,7,12,20). Finally, both the prologue and the letters to churches section are connected to the epilogue by the statement of Jesus that what he reveals to John will be transmitted by John to the churches through the intermediation of an angel (1:11; 2:1,8,12,18; 3:1,7,14 with 22:16).

Letters to Churches of Asia (2:1-3:22)

The letters to the churches echo imagery from the prologue and anticipate imagery in the last few chapters, usually the triumphant vision of 21:1-22:5 (*Ephesus*, 2:1 with 1:12-13,16 and 2:7 with 22:2; *Smyrna*, 2:8 with 1:5,8,11,17-18 and 2:11 with 20:14, 21:8; *Pergamos*, 2:12 with 1:16 but no specific image connecting with 21-22; *Thyatira*, 2:18 with 1:14-15, 2:27 with 19:15, and 2:28 with 22:16; *Sardis*, 3:1 with 1:4,16,20 and 3:5 with 20:12; *Philadelphia*, 3:7 with 1:18 and 3:12 with 21:2; *Laodicea*, 3:14 with 1:8,11, 22:12, and 3:21 with 1:8,18 and 3:20-21 with 19:9, 21:9, 22:3).

Divine Judgment on Godless Powers (4:1-20:15)

Chapters 4 through 20 constitute the lengthiest section of Revelation. Following the authoritative messages to the seven churches, each connected with the beginning of the book by images of the risen Christ figure and with its end by promises to overcomers which are seen fulfilled in the new heaven and earth, John sees a door opened in heaven and hears an invitation to enter and be shown "things which must be hereafter" (4:1). Thus begin the first scenes of God's heaven and his judgments.

The Sealed Book and the Seven Trumpets (4:1-9:21)

Immediately upon hearing "Come up hither," John is in the throne-room of heaven, the vantage point from which he will view the panorama of God's long-delayed judgment on the earth below in preparation for the coming righteous rule of God in the world he has created. John sees a sealed book in the hand of God on the throne, and when the "Lamb as it had been slain" is found worthy to take the book and begin to open the seven seals, terrible events begin to occur on the earth below. The seven seals are followed by seven trumpets, each of which signals fierce disasters and wars similar to those initiated by the seven seals. The unfolding of judgments on the earth is interrupted after the sixth trumpet; the suspense is heightened not only by the interrupting scene but also by the previous announcement that the last three trumpets represent three catastrophic "woes," and the third woe, to be initiated by the seventh trumpet, has not yet fallen.

The Open Book and the Seventh Trumpet (10:1-14:20)

While awaiting the seventh trumpet's sound, John sees a mighty angel with an open book which is offered to him to eat; as promised, the book is sweet in his mouth but nauseating in his stomach: like the Old Testament prophets (especially Ezekiel, who was also an imprisoned exile; cf. Ezek. 2:8-3:3), he must prophesy before "peoples, and nations, and tongues, and kings," without regard to whether the message is pleasant or harsh. Then in quick succession he is ordered to measure God's temple, sees the martyrdom and resurrection/ascension victory of two faithful witnesses, and hears the seventh trumpet. The "woe" announced by the trumpet is not revealed until heaven celebrates the imminent result of divine judgment on evil men and demons: God and Christ shall make earth's kingdoms God's kingdom and they "shall reign for ever and ever" (11:15). Another vision which precedes the woe of the seventh trumpet represents a dragon's (Satan's) attempts to conquer God, to destroy the Christ child brought forth by a woman (Israel), and to destroy the woman and her child; this vision is in the nature of a flashback to represent the origin of evil in the world and the triumph over evil accomplished through the incarnation, death, and resurrection of Jesus Christ (12:1-5). It presents in symbolic cameo the salvation history of the Hebrew Scriptures, of the Gospels, and of the present and future sufferings and ultimate victory of the Christian community (but see Keller 431-432). The full woe to the earth of the seventh trumpet is then revealed in the two beast-rulers, one from the sea and one from the earth, those powerful creatures who for a limited time will sum up in their cruel reign in the world all the bestial tyranny of godless power in man's history. The chief beast-ruler and his power structure, symbolized by the city of Babylon, will soon come to be "fully ripe" and God will put in his sickle of righteous judgment and reap (14:14-20).

The Seven Last Plagues, Babylon's Fall, and Heaven's Triumph (15:1-19:10)

The seven plagues, like the seven seals and the seven trumpets before them, are accompanied by victorious choruses in heaven that give assurance that God's kingdom has already triumphed in eternity and that the symbolic judging of the earth is simply working out in time what has been certainly ordained above and outside of time (5:9-14; 11:15-19; 15:2-8). The pouring out of the seventh vial is followed by great natural disasters, including an earthquake, and the destruction of Babylon the great, symbolized as a whore in purple, scarlet, and gold sitting on the beast of the seven heads and ten crowns. Kings and merchants lament Babylon's fall, but the saints and angels in heaven rejoice over her destruction

(18:21-19:5). The whore of Babylon sharply contrasts with the preceding figure of the godly, child-bearing "woman clothed with the sun [with] the moon under her feet, and . . . a crown of twelve stars" (12:11; cf. Gen. 37:9-10), who is protected by God. The section then closes with a description of the Lamb's wife, the church, to be seen soon as the New Jerusalem (21:9-10), a female figure in even sharper contrast with the whore of Babylon (Fiorenza, *Justice* 66 n.153); instead of purple robes, drunkenness, whoredom, association with a monstrous beast, here are clean linen, purity in marriage, association with the Lamb, and preparation for a marriage feast (18:3-6 with 19:7-9). The final scene (19:9-10) anticipates another in the epilogue: when John falls before him to worship, the angel forbids him and identifies himself as a "fellow servant" (19:10 with 22:8-9). Both scenes include the angel's admonition to "worship God" only and his self-identification with the prophets, but only the second (22:9) explicitly authenticates "the sayings of this book," the Revelation, with divine prophecy.

The Final Defeat of God's Enemies and the Judgment of the Dead (19:11-20:15)

The Word of God, described in images that recall the prologue (19:12 with 1:14 and 19:15 with 1:16), leads his heavenly armies in the total defeat of the two beasts (13:1,11) who have been used by Satan, the dragon, to persecute God's people on earth. Satan is bound for one thousand (Greek *chilias*)[8] years. During the thousand-year period, Christ rules over an earthly kingdom and his resurrected saints rule with him. Satan is then loosed, only to be permanently defeated and condemned forever to the place of torment where the beasts (the beast and his "false prophet") already are (20:1-3, 7-10). A great throne of judgment is established before which all the dead must stand to be judged from two books; only those written in the book of life are spared (20:12-15), since they were the ones who received grace to resist the beast (13:8).

God Rules a Union of Heaven and Earth Made New (21:1-22:5)

Now the Lord God omnipotent visibly reigns, as proclaimed earlier (19:6) over all creation now made new (21:5), and purged by cleansing judgments of all the disobedient (21:8,27). The new heaven needs no sun or moon, for the Lord God is the light of the new earth and there is no more night (21:23, 22:5). Like Eden, the new earth has abundant pure water and fruit from the tree of life and there is no sea and no sorrow (21:1,4; 22:1-2), but unlike pastoral Eden, the new earth has a holy city, the New Jerusalem, the symbol of all that is good as Babylon was the symbol of everything evil, a city founded on the tribes of Israel and the apostles of the church (21:12-14) to represent God's people of all the ages who "have the testimony of Jesus" (19:10) and thus are in "the bride, the Lamb's wife" (21:9). The presence of God and the resurrected Christ make a temple superfluous and God's people will serve him constantly (22:3).

Epilogue (22:6-21)

As indicated earlier, the epilogue reemphasizes the imminence of the apocalypse of Jesus Christ. The Christ himself speaks of his coming three times in the epilogue: "Behold [Surely], I come quickly" (22:7,12,20). And John, in spite of all the nauseating scenes of divine retribution in his book of prophecy, with the happy scenes of the New Jerusalem still before his eyes, responds with "let it be so" and a fervent prayer: "Amen. Even so, come, Lord Jesus" (22:20). This overview of Revelation as a whole is presented in topical outline form on page 79.

THEMATIC OUTLINE OF REVELATION[9]

PROLOGUE: The risen Jesus proclaims the imminent apocalypse and authorizes letters to the seven churches of Asia Minor (1:1-20).

LETTERS TO THE CHURCHES: Jesus Christ, known by images from the Prologue, to each church in turn pronounces praise and/or rebuke, promises to overcomers of evil, blessings associated with God's coming Kingdom, and exhortations to hear attentively (2:1-3:22).

THE APOCALYPSE—EVIL JUDGED AND DESTROYED: From the perspective of God's Throne in Heaven, John is shown scenes demonstrating that God controls and will soon judge Earth's evil powers in time, thus assuring the coming triumphant union of Heaven and Earth in eternity (4:1-20:15).

THE APOCALYPSE—ALL THINGS MADE NEW: God's triumphant Kingdom unites Heaven and Earth under the rule of God and the Lamb; saints are established in a happier Eden—New cosmic setting, New Heaven, New Earth, New Jerusalem, New undisturbed joy (21:1-22:5).

EPILOGUE: The imminence of the apocalypse is reaffirmed by John, by the angel, and by Jesus in imagery and phraseology repeated from all preceding sections: Prologue, Letters, and Apocalypse; final warnings, reemphasis on the Lord's coming, and prayer for grace for readers (22:6-21).

Chapter 7

Literary Analysis: The Major Divisions

Prologue and Letters (Chapters 1-3)

Prologue

As suggested earlier, the opening chapter of Revelation combines phraseology and structure which associate the passage with Christian epistolary form, particularly the letters of Paul and Peter (compare 1:4-7 with, e. g., Gal. 1:1-5, 1 Pet. 1:1-9); characteristically their letters open with identification of the writer and of his intended audience, followed by a blessing of grace and peace on the recipients and a doctrinal apostrophe to God or Christ or both. Further strengthening the epistolary association, even clearly apocalyptic characteristics of the prologue echo, albeit ironically, Paul's ecstatic, visionary experiences as related in his letters; for instance, the narrative in 2 Corinthians of Paul's rapture into paradise ("whether in the body . . . or out of the body, . . . God knoweth") to hear words unlawful to repeat (2 Cor. 12:3-4) is hinted at in John's relation of his experience "in the Spirit" on Patmos. The differences recall the Pauline experience by ironic contrast: Paul uses the modest evasion of an unnamed third-person character who is translated in the body or in the spirit (12:1-2) and hears words and sees visions unlawful to repeat in Paul's letter to Corinth; John uses the frank first person and, though he has his feet firmly on the sand of Patmos, he is unequivocally in the spirit and is commanded to write in a letter the words he hears and the visions he sees, not to one, but to *seven* churches. Like Paul, he too will soon be caught up to heaven, but unlike Paul, he will continue to receive orders to write almost all of what he sees and hears (the sole exception is what the seven thunders say, 10:4). As Beale describes John's portrait of the seven-horned lamb in 5:6 as an "implied ironic contrast with the ten-horned beast of Daniel 7[:7]" (323), I suggest that in his differences from Pauline practice, John's epistolary form also involves ironic contrast as structural allusion. Although Peter includes no visions in his letters, readers of Revelation would doubtless have been aware not only of Luke's story of Paul's confrontation with the risen Lord on the Damascus road (Acts 9:1-19, 22:6-16, 26:12-18) but also of his account of the Lord's vision given to Peter to overcome Peter's objection to bringing uncircumcised Gentiles into the church (Acts 10:9-16,28). Moreover, Peter's first epistle could justly be called an "apocalyptic letter" because of its use of the word *apokalupsis,* its eschatological content, and its parallels with Revelation and an apocalyptic letter of Baruch (Michaels 268-272). Thus associating the epistolary features of his apocalypse with letters of respected apostles who had written of Christ's second coming and had also themselves been recipients of heavenly visions, John gives his own apocalyptic experiences a kind of subtly effective apostolic authentication.

The extensive use of allusion, paraphrase, and even verbatim repetition of apocalyptic and prophetic passages in the opening chapter of Revelation is documented in the cross-references found in any standard edition of the Bible. The American Bible Society's Student Edition of the KJV and the Oxford Study Edition of the NEB agree, for example, in citing the following cross-references to prophets with apocalyptic tendencies: Rev.1:4-8—Dan.7:13, Zech.12:10; Rev.1:13-17—Dan.7:9-10,12-13; 10:5-6; Ezek.1:24-28; Isa.44:6, 48:12. The images found in these Hebrew prophets include the seven spirits before God's throne; a divine figure coming with the clouds; those who pierced their victim, seeing him alive again and wailing because of him; the transcendent son of man, hair white as wool and feet like fine brass; a divine voice like the sound of many waters; the visionary prophet's falling and being raised by a heavenly messenger; a divine proclamation of God as first and last. To these may be added the sun-like quality of the deity's countenance (1:16 [cf. 10:1] with Mal. 4:2) and the metaphor of a sword for the power of God's word (1:16 with Isa. 11:4, 49:2). Paulien has identified both thematic and structural parallels in Revelation as allusion to Ezekiel and Joel (42-43), and Willis lists quite a number of "specific passages . . . based on" Isaiah, Daniel, Zechariah, and Jeremiah as well as Ezekiel and Joel (232-238).

A structural association with the prophecy of Amos may be seen in the divinely ordained messages to seven specifically named churches, each letter except that to Philadelphia including a threat of judgment; Amos initiates his prophecy with a series of six "woes" to fall upon specific pagan peoples for their transgressions against God's word and his people, followed by final "woes" to fall upon God's own people for transgressing also against his word and the poor of the land. Since the Jews are constituted in two kingdoms, these judgments are pronounced separately against Judah and Israel, making a total of eight messages; the rhetorical effect is of seven messages, however, since Judah and Israel profess the same God and the same law (Amos 1:3-2:8). As Amos builds toward the shock effect of including the Jews in a list of Gentile peoples to be punished by God, John's concluding letter to Laodicea, described as "wretched, and miserable, and poor, and blind, and naked," though it sees itself as "rich and [in] need of nothing" (3:17), especially since it follows the commendatory letter to Philadelphia, carries the shock of surprise to this church as Amos's proclamation does to Israel and Judah, especially Israel, Amos's own homeland. If one is reminded of Amos in Revelation's structure of the letters, the reminder is appropriate to the content: as Amos moves from the inescapability of God's judgments to the blessings of restoration and renewal that will follow (Amos 9:1-15), Revelation's movement, both in individual letters and throughout the series, is similarly from warnings of judgment to promises of rewards for repentance and restoration.

The prologue and the letters to the seven churches are interlocked, as indicated earlier, by the images of Christ repeated from the prologue at the beginning of each letter. In addition, the epistolary statement in the prologue, "John to the seven churches which are in Asia" (1:4), the marks of epistolary genre already discussed, and the final farewell of the epilogue, also in epistolary style, merge the prologue with the entire apocryphal message as well as with the seven letters of Chapters 2 and 3, thus effectively making the entire book an apocalyptic letter to the churches. As Hellholm says, when the prologue calls all those blessed who read and hear this book, it makes Revelation "an Apocalypse addressed to a wider audience beyond the specific situation of the original letter [extending it] to an infinite set of anonymous receivers" (137). Furthermore, the effect of Christ's right hand being laid upon the prostrate John—the same hand which holds the seven stars, explained as "the angels [messengers, pastors] of the seven churches" (1:16-17,20)—is to authenticate John as the one divinely chosen to address the individual messengers in the preface to each letter, to recognize him as equivalent to those other messengers in the Lord's hand, and to form still another link between the prologue's inaugural vision, the letters, and the wider audience to be blessed by this prophecy (cf. 10:11).[10]

The Letters to the Seven Churches (2:1-3:22)

The significance of the number of Asian churches addressed has been variously interpreted. Why seven? Other churches existed in Asia Minor, at Colossae and Troas for instance (Col.1:1-3; Acts 20:6-7). And why Asia Minor? Asia Minor, perhaps, because tradition places John's apostolic and pastoral service in that region, especially in Ephesus, and a divine message through John would seem most appropriate and authentic if addressed to the Christian community with which John was known to have been most closely associated. As for the number seven, it is clearly a very important numerological symbol in the Book of

Revelation, and *seven* churches (represented already in the prologue as seven golden lampstands with their seven angels [messengers] represented by seven stars) prepare the reader for seven horns on the Lamb, seven seals on the little book, seven trumpets to announce divine judgments, seven thunders, and so on. Since the book is about the imminent end of the present world system, and seven speaks of finality, of completion, as in God's rest on the seventh day after creating the heavens and the earth (Gen. 2:2-3), seven seems symbolically appropriate for the number of churches to receive Christ's divine messages, including promises to come quickly (1:3 with 2:5, 16, 25; 3:3, 11), just prior to the end of the age. Perhaps also seven churches are chosen to represent a complete portrait of the various conditions obtaining in the churches of the time, or of any time.

If we look at a contemporary map of Asia at the end of the first century, we note that from John's location on Patmos, an island just off Miletus, Ephesus is north-northeast, and Smyrna and Pergamum are directly north of Ephesus; Thyatira is southeast of Pergamum, directly south is Sardis, and on a southeasterly line from Sardis are Philadelphia and Laodicea: the churches in the order addressed in the seven letters form a rough oval on the map with the third and fourth, Pergamum and Thyatira, forming the top curve of the oval and the first and the last, Ephesus and Laodicea standing on either side of the open bottom of the oval. The circle is not closed, but the elongated oval figure formed by the churches reinforces the idea that a series of seven represents a complete portrait of the spiritual condition of the churches ranging from faithful zeal to complacent sloth.[11]

Some interpreters have seen the seven churches as representative of seven phases of the church age, stretching from Pentecost to the Second Coming: Ephesus, according to such a reading, is most like the church of John's day, and a general deterioration of spiritual obedience coupled with increasing materialism and corruption of apostolic doctrine culminates in the lukewarm spiritual bankruptcy of the Laodicean church in the days just before the return of Christ.

Such a reading, however, does not account for some of the severest condemnations falling upon Thyatira and Sardis though they precede Philadelphia, the church threatened less and given more comforting promises than churches earlier in the sequence; nor does it take into account the gracious appeal, almost supplication, of Jesus for renewed fellowship with the Laodicean church (3:19-20) compared with his harsher words to churches preceding Laodicea: Ephesus (2:5), Pergamos (2:16), Thyatira (2:22), and Sardis (3:3) (Roloff 452). Guthrie is doubtless correct in repudiating as "non-historical" (71) a rationale based on ecclesiastical decline for the order of the churches.

Since the letters to the churches are closely uniform in structure, any variation stands out. Each letter consists of the following parts (asterisks and church names indicate exceptions), in the same order unless noted:

(1) admonition to John to write to the angel of the church;

(2) identification of the risen Lord as source of the message, using imagery from the inaugural vision;

(3) message proper, consisting of:

(a) "I know [Greek, *oida*] thy works";

(b) praise (*Laodicea); Sardis after rebuke;

(c) rebuke (*Smyrna, *Philadelphia);

(d) threat echoing identification image (*Smyrna, *Philadelphia);

(4) exhortation to hear the Spirit [for the first three churches, exhortation *precedes* promise; for the final four, exhortation *follows* promise];[12]

(5) promise foreshadowing images from the new age portrayed at book's end.

As indicated above, Laodicea receives no praise and Smyrna and Philadelphia no rebuke (though the praise of the latter for "a little strength," 3:8, is faint indeed).

Since these two churches are also spared any threat, though their enemies are threatened and the churches promised vindication (2:10, 3:9), and Philadelphia's promises are more abundant (three promises precede the expected formulaic promise anticipating the future, 3:8-10), these churches conflated seem closer to an ideal paradigm than Ephesus, whose initial position might suggest otherwise. Because Sardis is rebuked *before* being praised, the selectivity of the praise comes as no surprise: only a few have kept themselves pure and the phrase "even in Sardis" suggests a situation in the church as a whole worse than any other except Laodicea (3:4), a suggestion confirmed by the statement that the church is already dead despite its reputation for being alive (3:1). Finally, a comparative analysis of the letters suggests that, as the only two churches spared threats in the imagery of divine judgment from the prologue (though both are warned of threats posed by demonically inspired human enemies and promised divine vindication), Smyrna and Philadelphia, the second and the sixth churches among seven and the only churches not charged with tolerating apostate doctrines or practices, provide a standard against which churches wishing to please the risen and soon-to-appear head of the church may measure themselves most beneficially.

These comments may be illustrated graphically as follows: churches number two and six are treated positively—1 *2* 3 4 5 *6* 7. The two churches which provide the extremest negative examples, on the other hand, are Sardis and Laodicea, the fifth and seventh churches respectively. Not only does the content of the text suggest such a classification with Smyrna and Philadelphia at the positive end of the spectrum and Sardis and Laodicea at the negative end, the pattern of repetition of imagery from the prologue to identify the risen Lord in each case suggests confirmation of such a qualitative polarization. Although Hemer warns against "mere priority of order" as meaningful in relating Revelation 1 to Revelation 2-3 (17), there does appear to be a correlation between the negative or positive terms of Christ's epistolary messages and the original position in the prologue of the self-identifying images he repeats in the letters.

The following display will clarify the point.

churches in order of text	*images in order of prologue*
1-Ephesus	3-seven lamps (1:13)
2-Smyrna	6-first/last; dead/alive (1:17-18)
3-Pergamos	5-two-edged sword in mouth (1:16)
4-Thyatira	4-eyes of fire; feet of brass (1:14-15)
5-Sardis	1-seven spirits (1:4)
6-Philadelphia	7-key of Death [David] (1:18)
7-Laodicea	2-faithful witness which was (1:5)

Christ's identification to Smyrna and Philadelphia employs images from the prologue in closest proximity to the series of letters, images that give assurance and confirmation of faith (2:6 and 6:7 above); his identification to Sardis and Laodicea reaches farthest back into the prologue for images that probe and question sincerity (5:1 and 7:2 above). The prologue position of the identification image of Christ when he addresses Thyatira (4:4), especially given the church's central position in the series (three churches on either side), corresponds with the pivotal nature of the content: this church is praised almost as warmly as Smyrna and Philadelphia except for their toleration of a prophetess who points forward to the great whore of the apocalypse, and overcomers are promised rulership with an iron rod over the ungodly, an anticipation of the millennial reign which follows the downfall of Babylon (17:4-5,14; 19:15; 20:4). Another patterning feature serves to set off Thyatira as a center, or at least a turning point, in the series: the first three churches are first told to hear the Spirit and then given a promise for overcomers, while the last four churches are given promises for overcomers and then told to hear the Spirit.[13] As the fourth church, the one with which this structural shift of pattern begins and also the church to receive the lengthiest letter (Kirby 204), Thyatira appears as the modular center of the series of seven.

To sum up, the structure described may be illustrated by the following series with the numbers representing the letters to the churches in the order given in the text (1:11 and 2:1-3:22): 1=Ephesus, 2=Smyrna, 3=Pergamos, 4=Thyatira, 5=Sardis, 6=Philadelphia, and 7=Laodicea.

1   2   3   4   5   6   7

Churches 2 and 6 (Smyrna and Philadelphia) as those most positively addressed stand out in their next-to-first and next-to-last positions; church 4 (Thyatira), for reasons given above, represents the hinge of the series; churches 5 and 7 (Sardis and Laodicea) as those most negatively addressed lose stature by comparison with the outstanding church which separates them (Philadelphia), and churches 1 and 3, while their spiritual standing is strong compared with churches 5 and 7 (Sardis and Laodicea), serve as foils to the higher status of church 2 (Smyrna). While I grant that this description is largely subjective, the textual grouping of objective details leads to the conclusion that position in the series has meaning.

Although the arrangement of parts within the series which dominates the opening chapters of Revelation is quite different from the disposition of the series of narratives which initiates Daniel, the interrelating of parts within each series, and also the interrelating of both parts and the entire series which they compose within the book as a whole, is carried out with the same kind of careful artistic and rhetorical structuring by both authors. The reader may wish to compare the diagram on page 119 with the figure illustrating the structure of Daniel on the same page.

Although he makes no connection between Daniel and Revelation, I find Aune's identification of the form of the seven letters in the Apocalypse as "mixed genre" composed of royal edict and salvation-judgment oracle (183) especially interesting in the light of Daniel's narratives with their royal edicts and dream-inspired judgment oracles. The rationale Aune attributes to John echoes significant resonances from Daniel's narrative theme: "John has consciously employed the form of the royal or imperial edict. . . to emphasize. . .that Christ is the true king in contrast to the Roman emperor who is both a clone and tool of Satan" (204).

As Nebuchadnezzar proclaimed upon being restored from his bestial state, God's "dominion is everlasting. . .in heaven and [in] earth. [His] works are truth and his ways judgment; and those that walk in pride he is able to abase" (Dan. 4:35,37).

The Apocalypse—Evil Judged and Destroyed (4:1-20:15)

As the apocalypse proper begins with John's translation to heaven itself in Chapter 4, again there are interlocking features connecting this new section with what has gone before: the phrases "after this" and "the things which must be hereafter" (4:1) call to mind the admonition of the risen Lord to John in the prologue to write not only of what he has seen and of what is mysteriously present in the inaugural vision but also of "the things which shall be hereafter" (1:19); the voice like a trumpet that now calls him to enter the open door in heaven (4:1) is the "great voice, as of a trumpet" who ordered the letters to the churches in the prologue (1:10-11); John's dazzling vision of God's throne in heaven includes characteristics already seen in the epistolary salutation and apostrophe—"the seven Spirits of God" (now also associated with the seven lamps) are there before the throne (1:4 with 4:5; cf. 3:1) and on the throne of the universe is seated him "which is, and which was, and which is to come" (1:4; cf. 1:8,11,17), now described as him who "was, and is, and is to come" (4:8). But while these features common to both sections preserve the continuity of the book, they are so overshadowed by the startling new sights and sounds John describes as to go almost unnoticed.

Suddenly the Almighty Father is not a majestic abstraction to be worshipped in quiet contemplation, he is (like his risen Son) a glorious presence, essentially inexpressible and therefore describable only in the similes of human language: his brilliant appearance "is like a jasper and a sardine stone [cornelian, NEB]," the throne is encircled by an emerald-like rainbow, symbol of peace between heaven and earth, and yet vibrant with ominous sights and sounds: lightning flashes and thunder claps (4:4-5; cf. Exod. 19:16). Twenty-four seats, each occupied by white-clad (cf. 3:4,5,18), gold-crowned elders surround the throne (4:4; cf. 2:10, 3:11,21), and in a central position before the throne are "four beasts" (living creatures), each with a distinctive face (lion, ox, man, eagle, in later tradition symbols of Mark, Luke, Matthew, and John respectively), six-winged and blessed with the power of God-exalting song as were the seraphim in Isaiah's vision (4:6-8; cf. Isa. 6:2-3; Ezek. 1:5-10,10:14). As John watches, the beasts glorify God as the Eternal Holy One and the elders praise him as the Eternal Creator who is "worthy. . . to receive glory and honor and power [authority]" (4:11), foreshadowing the next scene to come in which this worthy God, finding no other creature in the universe to be worthy to receive the book he holds in his hand, yields the book to the "Lion of the tribe of Judah, the Root of David, . . . [the] Lamb as it had been slain" (5:5-6) as "worthy to take the book, and to open the seals thereof" (5:9) because he redeemed to God by his blood a mighty throng "out of every kindred, and tongue, and people, and nation" (5:9). Minear remarks that "the essential key to every vision of the *Apocalypse* is . . . the truth that a creature whose contingency and mortality is signified in the form of a slaughtered Lamb [is] exalted to the position of power at God's right hand" (234) and, paradoxically, in that position he has the sovereignty of the Lion of the tribe of Judah (Rev. 5:5).[14]

Seeing the figure on the heavenly throne, in his hand a scroll rolled up and sealed, and hearing an angel shout the challenge, "Who is worthy to open the book, and to loose the seals thereof?" (5:2), John, concluding that no one in the universe can be found worthy, is emotionally overcome and begins to weep. John's distraught state at six points in his visionary experiences is comparable to Daniel's emotional state in six situations: compare Rev.1:17 with Dan. 10:8-10; Rev. 5:4 with Dan. 4:19; Rev. 10:8-10 with Dan. 7:15,28; Rev. 17:6-7,18 with Dan. 8:15-27; Rev. 19:9-10 with Dan. 10:5-11,15-19; Rev. 22:8-9 with Dan.12:8-9.

Although these scenes in the two apocalypses are not close parallels, their common features suggest that the books in which they appear share some common assumptions about divine-human intercourse in apocalyptic. For instance: divine epiphanies can traumatize even strong human beings; angelic messengers show sympathetic concern for those receiving revelations; the recipient of apocalyptic visions may identify so completely with them that the spectator becomes participant; the sense of responsibility for a divine message humbles and staggers the prophet; in contact with supernatural figures the prophet cannot differentiate unaided between deity and fellow-servant.

As we have seen, John's tears are soon dried, for when the crucified and risen Christ, the Lamb, is found worthy to open the scroll and remove the seals, all heaven bursts into anthems of praise and thanksgiving for the worthiness of the Lamb, followed by a universal chorus of every created thing singing praises to God and the Lamb. All heaven is represented by the twenty-four elders and the four living creatures; they accompany their song on golden harps and they each have vials of incense symbolizing the prayers of the saints (5:8; cf. Psalm 141:2). The content of many of those prayers is soon made clear with the opening of the fifth seal: martyrs of the ages pray for judgment on the godless world and for the avenging of their blood (6:9-10), and God will answer their prayers (8:3-5).

The Lamb's opening of the scroll's first seal results from what precedes and sets in motion interconnected and causally related visions which represent an ineluctable forward flow of divinely initiated events toward the apocalypse of Jesus Christ "which must shortly come to pass" (1:1); that is, despite some intercalated sections, the entire river of the apocalypse flows steadily from its source in the inaugural vision to its opening into the vast expanse of an eternally united heaven and earth where "there shall be no more curse" (22:3; cf. Zech. 14:11). The judgments launched by the seven seals are paralleled and elaborated on by the judgments initiated by the two succeeding series of sevens: the seventh seal introduces seven angels to sound seven trumpets to announce seven judgments, following which seven angels pour from seven vials the seven last plagues on the earth (8:2-9:21, 10:15, 15:1-20:15).   Between the sixth and seventh seals two visions are interpolated: the sealing of 144,000 Israelites, 12,000 from each of the twelve tribes, and the white-robed multitude before the throne and the Lamb, a multitude described as having been delivered from "great tribulation" and now knowing complete joy (7:1-17).

A similar interpolation[15] appears between the sixth and seventh trumpets: a "mighty angel" (imagery suggests the risen Lord—compare 10:1 with 1:7,15,16b; 4:3) with a second scroll commissions John afresh as a prophet, reveals that the seventh trumpet will initiate the completion of the "mystery of God" (10:1-11), and in dramatic narration presents two witnesses who, after prophesying to the accompaniment of miracles, are martyred, resurrected, and assumed into heaven (11:1-14; cf. 1 Kings 17:1, Exod. 7:17-19). The seventh trumpet then sounds and the heavenly anthems proclaim the time has come for God to judge the earth and establish his everlasting kingdom in heaven and earth (11:15-19).

Now that the seventh trumpet has sounded, before the first vial of plagues is poured out another seemingly parenthetical passage intervenes. John sees wonders in heaven, in the sea, and in the earth: to the figures of the mighty angel with the little book and the two witnesses are added "a woman clothed with the sun," a "great red dragon," and two beasts, one from the sea and one from the earth, *seven* figures in all (12:1-13:18).[16] Another three visions appear: a host of 144,000 "redeemed from the earth" sing a new song before God's throne, three angelic heralds fly over the earth (announcing respectively the "everlasting gospel," the fall of Babylon, and everlasting punishment for those who "worship the beast and his image"), and the "Son of man" and "another angel" wield sickles with which they begin to "reap . . . the harvest of the earth" (14:1-20). Now the seven angels issue from the temple of God in heaven, ready to empty the vials "full of the wrath of God" (15:6-7).

The seven last plagues on the earth and its atmosphere culminate in the seventh which causes an earthquake to raze "the cities of the nations," chief of which is Babylon (15:1-16:21); the judgment and fall of Babylon, imaged as "the great whore," symbol of the commercial exploitation of humanity and the persecution of the saints by a godless world system, is described more fully than any other one judgment included in Revelation (17:1-18:24). (Two full chapters for Babylon's destruction stand in sharp contrast to the final judgment of Satan and the two beasts, dispatched in one verse, 20:10.)

In a work with so many repetitive patterns, the intervening visions between the sixth and seventh seals (7:1-17) and the sixth and seventh trumpets (10:1-11:14) lead the reader to expect a space between the sixth and seventh plagues—but there is none (16:12-21), as though to symbolize the accelerating pace of divine judgment once the process draws near its close. The "mighty angel" with the second book has sworn "that there shall be time no longer" [literally, "no more delay"] when events announced by the seventh trumpet shall begin to unfold (10:6-7). The seven last plagues spring from the seventh trumpet as the trumpets sprang from the seventh seal; but then they move more swiftly to their conclusion than any preceding series, and they form the only numbered series of judgments that moves from start to finish in unbroken narrative (16:1-17: 18 verses compared with 29 for the seven trumpets [8:6-20, 11:15] and 22 verses for the seven seals [6:1-16, 8:1-5]). There is also an extended exultation lingering over the final effects of the seventh plague, the fall of Babylon (17:1-18:24), a unique appendage among the series of sevens.

This lingering exultation over fallen Babylon—though intermingled are moving expressions of regret for its fall, both by those selfishly lamenting the loss of their investments of power and commerce (18:9-19) and by heavenly voices describing the disappearance from the city of music, art, and *joie de vivre* (18:22-23a)—has troubled readers as reflecting an envious relish for savage vengeance by the saints on their enemies (Collins "Persecution" 747; Lawrence 63, 157). At least Collins, though seeing the "tremendous potential for real psychological and social evil" in vengeance and envy, concedes that Revelation "limits vengeance and envy to the imagination and clearly rules out violent deeds" by the saints (747). And in another work, she examines the exultation over Babylon as an Aristotelian catharsis, i.e., the arousal through vicarious experience of powerful feelings of desire for revenge in order to bring about a purgation and reduction of these feelings to a manageable and coherent order *(Crisis* 144-156).

While I agree that the analogy with the catharsis of a tragic play is an apt one, I see as well an ironic reversal of the story of Jonah and Nineveh in the account of the mourners for Babylon. Jonah keeps a vigil outside repentant Nineveh and laments the city's being mercifully spared instead of suffering the destruction that Jonah, at God's command, has pronounced on the sinful city (Jonah 3:10-4:5). As Jonah sees it, God is unreasonably merciful to Nineveh and Jonah is angry (Jonah 4:2-3). In Revelation the kings, merchants, and mariners "stand afar off" and lament the destruction of unrepentant Babylon by a just God (Rev. 18:9-19), whom they see as arbitrarily vengeful. The heavenly voices in Revelation rejoice over Babylon's fall as Jonah had hoped to exult over Nineveh's before being disappointed, even outraged, by God's forgiveness. Thus the Apocalypse, while seemingly applauding in an unqualified way the divine destruction of earthly evil, alludes to a book of Hebrew prophecy which ends with God's patient efforts to make the prophet realize experientially that since God takes no pleasure in the destruction of his creatures, his prophet should not do so either; he should instead rejoice that sinners have repented. The major difference, of course, is that Babylon has not repented and must therefore be judged. Still the condemnation of the city for being stained with "the blood of prophets, and of saints, and of all that were slain" (18:24) comes at the close of a poignant catalogue of the evidences of joyful human habitation that have forever disappeared from the city's streets and homes and marketplaces (18:22-23a).

"After these things" John envisions the heavenly throne-room once again and hears the saints, represented by the elders and the living creatures, also exulting over the just fall of Babylon and anticipating the marriage of the Lamb

and his bride and the wedding celebration to follow (19:1-10). First, however, the
risen Christ must vanquish the godless forces of earth and hell and John sees
visions of that great victory, of the final defeat of the devil and his cohorts, and
of the judgment of the dead of the ages (19:11-20:15). John's description of the
judgment phase of the apocalypse is accomplished; there remains only his vision
of the complete renewal of creation and its union with the Creator as a new
heaven and new earth in which the redeemed enjoy forever the just fruits of the
apocalypse of Jesus Christ.

The Apocalypse—All Things Made New (21:1-22:5)

Connectives with preceding sections, especially the most proximate one,
continue to be a structural strategy in this penultimate literary division of
Revelation. The passing away of the first heaven and earth to make way for the
new (21:1) has been prepared for and given appropriate occasion in the scene
establishing a "great-white throne" of judgment for the dead (20:11), the descent
of the new Jerusalem (21:2) adorned as a bride is foreshadowed in the heavenly
Alleluia praising God's sovereign rule (19:6-7), the disappearance of all offenders
into the "second death" (21:8) harks back to the opposite of the resurrection to
life described by this phrase (20:6,14), and God's union with the faithful in his
temple and wiping away all tears from their eyes (21:3-4) fulfills the vision of the
redeemed from "great tribulation" and the angelic interpretation to John
(7:13-17). There remains on the scene one of the seven angels who inflicted the
last plagues (15:1), but now his mission and message involve not stern retributive
judgment, as when he revealed Babylon as the great whore (17:1), but grace and
peace and beauty, initiated by his revelation of "the Lamb's wife" (21:9ff.);
instead of destroying the world's cities and polluting the earth and its water and
air (16:4,17,19), the angel takes pleasure in revealing the magnitude of the
magnificent capital city[17] and showing John the purity and health-insuring
environment of the new world (21:15-22:5). This new world has none of the
features that have been symbolic or actual manifestations and/or results of man's

alienation from and rebellion against God: the sea (21:1); loneliness (21:3); sorrow, pain, and death (21:4); thirst (21:6); evil predators (21:8);[18] divisive places of worship (21:22); barren trees (22:2); judgment by or separation from God (22:3); darkness (21:25); light from any source other than God (22:5). All of these phenomena appear in Revelation's earlier scenes and images and are, of course, the common lot of mankind in any climate or culture, but in this utopian vision of God's union of heaven and earth in a new creation all such things are forever banished.

As pointed out earlier, the direct and unmediated speech of God on his throne to John in this passage is unique in Revelation (21:5-8). The risen Christ as "Son of man" or portrayed as a "mighty angel" speaks to John at times without angelic mediation (e.g., 1:17ff, 10:9), but not the enthroned Almighty Father. The NEB Oxford note to v. 5 says, "Only here and in 1:8 does God himself speak" (331). Apparently 1:8 is determined to be God's, rather than Christ's, speech because of the designation "Almighty" since every other epithet in the verse is applied to the risen Christ elsewhere in Revelation. Such a precise distinction of God from Christ on the basis of the ascription "Almighty" is difficult to support; for instance, the battle in which the Word of God, clearly Christ, will tread "the winepress of the fierceness and wrath of Almighty God" is spoken of earlier as "the battle of that great day of God Almighty" (19:15 with 16:14), yet God does not descend from his throne to the battle but acts through his Son, whose swift victory is evidence of almightiness, whether his own or his Father's. There is in 1:8 no other textual clue to distinguish the speaker as God the Father; in 21:5, however, the clear statement is that "he that sat upon the throne" speaks. Jesus Christ, the Lamb, is spoken of as standing "in the midst of the throne" (5:6), not sitting on the throne, though the river of life is described "proceeding out of the throne of God *and of the Lamb*" (22:1, italics added). I can see nothing structural or contextual in Rev. 1 that would justify identifying 1:8 as an insertion of God the Father's speech; in Rev. 22, on the other hand, the structural shift from mediation to immediacy, the reinforcement of divine-human intimacy in the newly united heaven and earth, and the statement that the speaker sits on the throne all support God himself as the speaker.

The rhetorical effect of this departure from the expected pattern of communication between heaven and the prophet is to enhance the emphasis in the text on the new intimacy of divine-human relationships to be enjoyed in the new universal order of God's kingdom: "God *himself* shall be with" humankind and personally "wipe away all tears" (21:3b-4, italics added).

The Epilogue (22:6-21)

The epilogue is perhaps the most difficult section of Revelation in which to identify clearly who is speaking and where each speech begins and ends. The difficulty of attributing speeches has been seen by Jacques Derrida as a characteristic feature of apocalyptic. He points out that in Revelation there is no secure indication within the text of either mediation or tone and argues that indeterminacy of tone and address is the hallmark of apocalyptic literature; when we can no longer tell who is speaking or writing and in what tone of voice, we are reading or hearing apocalypse. Derrida cites as an example Revelation 22:17, the threefold "Come," and says that the word "can be said [intoned] in almost every possible tone, every possible register of voice" (94). Some identifications can be made, however, without doubt: the first speaker is one of the angels who inflicted the seven last plagues on the earth (15:1; 16:1ff; 17:1; 19:9; 21:9,15; 22:1, 6) and his speech includes 22:6. Just as clearly, the angel speaks 22:10-11, though 22:11 repeats verbatim the words of Jesus Christ in 1:3b: "the time is at hand." But does he also speak verse 7?

> Behold, I come quickly. Blessed is he that keepeth the sayings of the prophecy of this book.

Since these statements of 22:7 echo the substance of 1:3, which is presented as a message from Jesus Christ through his angel to John, the content of the words is Christ's, whether they are spoken by the angel or by Jesus Christ himself. That

John, remembering the words in the context of the inaugural vision, falls down to worship may indicate that he mistakes the sound of the spoken words as coming from the mouth of the risen Jesus himself, and he must be corrected by the angel. A similar situation occurs in 19:9; "Blessed are they which are called to the marriage supper of the Lamb," though spoken by an angel, is mistaken by John for the words of Christ himself and he falls prostrate to worship (cf. Matt. 22:1ff and Luke 14:6ff.).

The mistake, it soon appears, is an understandable one, since Jesus apparently actually speaks in 22:12-13, though the text includes no clear attribution. Christ certainly does speak in 22:16:

> I Jesus have sent mine angel to testify unto these things in the churches.
> I am the root and the offspring of David, and the bright and morning star.

But whether or not he speaks verses 17-18 is indeterminable, though the final invitation of verse 17, following the invitation of Spirit, bride (church), and hearer of this prophecy, would be most appropriate coming directly from the Lord Jesus (cf. Isa. 55:1; John 4:13-14, 7:37-38).

> And let him that is athirst come. And whosoever will, let him take of the
> water of life freely.

Finally, the dialogue preceding the closing prayer of the book may be read equally well as the final statement of Christ to John followed by John's immediate response *or* as John's repetition of the remembered substance of Christ's "the time is at hand" (1:3) coupled with his "Amen" (1:18; cf. 3:14) followed by a response given by John as an appropriate prayer so be it, Lord (NEB and NRSV [Oxford] read "Amen. Come, Lord Jesus!" Thus the "amen" is connected with John's response, not with Christ's statement).

> Surely I come quickly: Amen.
> Even so, come, Lord Jesus.

Literary Influence

George Eliot, whose comment on Daniel's importance is quoted in Part I, uses the structures and themes of the Apocalypse in her novel, *Romola,* as she had used Daniel in *Daniel Deronda.* As Carpenter and Landow point out, she continued to use apocalyptic materials, following the interpretations of such theological writers on Revelation as E. B. Elliott as well as her own, in later novels such as *Felix Holt* and *Middlemarch* (301, 307-308). Revelation's hold on the imagination of literary artists and the tendency of its images and structures to emerge in their work have a long history in English literature before the nineteenth century and the story continues even today—Alastair Fowler, for instance, refers to an "Apocalyptic Group" of opaque British poets in the 1940's and 50's; apparently they were sufficiently opaque as to be widely unknown (371). But also among those who have reflected Revelation and apocalypticism in their works are some of the most justly famous who have "pleased many and pleased long."

In the middle ages the Gawain-poet (so named for *Sir Gawain and the Green Knight,* also called the Pearl-poet) in his dream-vision *Pearl* associates his narrator with St. John the Divine in his culminating vision of the Heavenly Jerusalem. The narrator makes his way up a jewelled river (based on the River of Life) to the Holy City and sees a procession of pearl maidens (instead of the male virgins of Revelation) led by a seven-horned Lamb as a bridegroom with his bride; the Lamb is bleeding from his side, as the narrator conflates the "lamb as it had been slain" from Revelation 5 with the Lamb who is married to the holy city and is enthroned in Revelation 21. The Dreamer sees among the Lamb's pearl-maidens his own lost pearl, but the occasional focus of the narrator does not detract from the poem's effect of "bridg[ing] the distance between human life and heavenly glory . . .with dramatic boldness" worthy of John's own visions (Fielding 16).

In the Renaissance both Shakespeare and Milton reflect the Apocalypse in many of their works. Hassel has shown, for instance, that Shakespeare's *Richard III* surrounds Richard by "intimations of apocalypse and eschatology" as he is associated by allusion to Revelation with Antichrist and Richmond with Christ (35, 38). And Fitts demonstrates that Revelation's "woman clothed with the sun," who must flee to the wilderness for protection and the dragon who pursues her (Chapter 12), as interpreted by earlier and contemporary commentators, becomes in *Cymbeline* a parallel for Imogen and her nemesis Iachimo, thus placing the human story within a much broader context of apocalyptic symbolism (2-3, 43). As a final Shakespearean example, Wittreich has shown that *King Lear* is permeated throughout with "the ambience of apocalypse" (188) from such explicit references as Lear's question, "Is this the promis'd end?" (186) through the trumpet blasts that bring the play to a close (188) and the wiping away of tears (191) to a wholeness of vision that is "the sardonic apocalypse," a vision of a future to be "effected . . . by man himself" (195).

That Milton saw Revelation as not only an important biblical book of prophecy but also as a work of literary art is well known. In *the Reason of Church Government* he apostrophizes the Apocalypse as "the majestic image of a high and stately tragedy, shutting up and intermingling her solemn scenes and acts with a seven-fold chorus of hallelujahs and harping symphonies" (Hughes 669), and Ryken has shown that his greatest poem, *Paradise Lost*, manifests a "unified apocalyptic vision" *(Apocalyptic Vision,* Chapter 8) throughout, a unity composed of most of the artistic techniques apocalyptic writings, including Revelation, employ. And the late Dean Patrides ("Apocalyptic Configurations" passim) discusses with his usual grace and comprehensiveness both the great importance of Revelation's influence in Milton's poetry and prose and the need to avoid exaggerated claims of that influence, since Milton is nothing if not universally eclectic and transformative in his choice of raw materials.

William Blake, another writer and artist who transformed all he drew upon for his own peculiar visions, including the Bible and Milton's poems, was "intensely affected by the language and imagery of St. John's Revelation" (Meyer 148). He executed eleven watercolor illustrations for Revelation, among them two almost overpowering conceptions of the "woman clothed with the sun" (Rev. 12:1) and the dragon. These pictures, now in the Brooklyn Museum and the National Gallery, Washington, are reproduced and described in Meyer (149-150), whose article also reproduces Blake's illustration of the mighty angel casting Satan into the bottomless pit (Rev. 20:1-2; 151). According to Hersey, Blake's "Four Zoas" are "suggested by the four beasts around the heavenly throne" in Revelation 4 (350). Whatever the text, however, for Blake as for Milton, art does not simply represent or echo biblical texts; the color, line, and word embody personal philosophy and vision.

In the twentieth century Yeats, Auden, Eliot, Faulkner, and Percy are writers who sometimes are apocalyptic in their literary art: Yeats in "A Vision," Auden (quietly) in "For the Time Being," Eliot (also quietly but powerfully) in "The Wasteland," Faulkner in *As I Lay Dying,* and Walker Percy in *Lancelot* and others. But perhaps the writer most centrally influenced in her vision of wayward and twisted human life in a universe ultimately controlled by an all-powerful God of judgment and salvation is Flannery O'Connor. Violent atrocity and vengeance become necessary to cleansing and wholeness in her apocalyptic world. One example is her story "Revelation," in which the violence is not physical but verbal—she is called by someone she considers an inferior an "old wart hog"—yet it has a cleansing and redemptive effect on Ruby Turpin, the self-righteous Pharisee and central intelligence of the story, and brings about for her an apocalyptic vision of "white trash, clean for the first time in their lives, and bands of black[s] in white robes, and battalions of freaks and lunatics shouting and clapping" (quoted in Perisho 6), an ironic reflection of the heavenly saints in Revelation 7:14-17 who have "washed their robes, and made them white in the

]blood of the Lamb'' (7:14). O'Connor's story is even structured in a chiastic arrangement of four scenes (Perisho 5), in the last of which Mrs. Turpin stares into her pig-pen ''as if through the very heart of mystery,'' and then lifts her head to see in the sky the vision of the redeemed (Perisho 6). One may observe in this short story a microcosm of O'Connor's ability skillfully to integrate into her novels the imagery, symbolism, and structure of Revelation, particularly *Wise Blood* and *The Violent Bear It Away* (see Kessler).

McGinn reminds us that ''Revelation is a great symbolic work of literature, more of a poem than a philosophical or historical treatise'' (''Revelation'' 539), and the book's perennial appeal to writers and artists is a tribute to its generative power. As Paul Pritchard has said,

> The Apocalypse is alien to Western habits of thought and, thus, is especially a mystery in our day. Nonetheless, partly for its mistily evident grandeur of vision, it repays careful, cautious study. It reminds modern man that the mystic's vision transcends ours yet is valid. Truth may be apprehended by other than rational or imaginative means as ordinarily experienced. (315)

PART III

DANIEL AND REVELATION

O Lord, . . . let thine anger . . . be turned away
From thy city Jerusalem, thy holy mountain.
(Daniel 9:16)

And I John saw the holy city, New Jerusalem,
Coming down from God out of heaven.
(Revelation 21:2)

Chapter 8

Shape as Meaning

The Book of Daniel closes with the prophet receiving a heavenly command to "shut up the words, and seal the book, even to the time of the end" (12:4); the Book of Revelation closes with a heavenly command to John to seal *not* the sayings of the prophecy of this book: for the time is at hand" (22:10, italics added). In the context of the command to Daniel, "the man clothed in linen," described earlier in terms very like the figure of the risen Lord Jesus in Revelation's prologue (Dan. 10:5-6 with Rev. 1:13-15), standing on the river with his hands held toward heaven, swears that the "time of the end" will be for "a time, times, and a half" (Dan. 12:7), and when Daniel, not understanding, asks, "O my Lord, what shall be the end of these things?" he is told again that "the words are closed up and sealed till the time of the end" (Dan. 12:8-9). We shall return to this angel later. In the immediate context of the command to John, the prophet hears both an angel and Christ speak to him, the former stating that "the time is at hand," the latter saying, "Behold, I come quickly" (Rev. 22:10,12); this emphasis on imminent expectation, unlike the prophesied but indefinitely delayed "time of the end" in Daniel, a time which must await certain developments in human history, removes any need for John to question exactly when the "short time" will occur in which God will destroy Satan and his followers and usher in his eternal kingdom: suddenly, at any time, just as John heard without warning the "voice. . .as a trumpet [saying] 'Come up hither'"

(Rev. 4:1; cf. 1:10), the moment will arrive. Revelation shares this concept of an imminent return of Christ to begin the establishment of the kingdom of heaven, a return not predicated upon previous historical events, with Paul's letters: announced by a trumpet blast, the Lord will suddenly descend to raise the dead believers and gather the living to himself (1 Thess. 4:16-17; 1 Cor. 15:51-52; cf. Mk. 13:32-37, Mt. 24:36-44, Lk. 17:26-37).[19]

The two apocalypses are, then, in spite of their many similarities, radically different in outlook: Daniel looks forward to a distant future in which God's kingdom will triumph after certain historical developments occur culminating in a beast-ruler "of fierce countenance, and understanding dark sentences [who] shall stand up . . . against the Prince of princes [only to be] broken without hand" (Dan. 8:23,25; cf. 2:34,43), while Revelation portrays an imminent coming of God's kingdom that is not dependent on any historical chain of events or the rise of a particular series of world rulers to prepare for it or initiate it. As Paul explained to the Thessalonians, however, although no one can accurately predict the arrival of "the day of Christ," there are predicted events that will immediately follow that day—e.g., the rise of the "man of sin" (the beast) and his blasphemous actions; therefore, one can be sure that the return of Christ has not yet occurred if these events have not yet begun to unfold (2 Thess. 2:1-10). These predictions are drawn by Revelation from Daniel; but while in the earlier prophet those events were understood as *preconditions* to the breaking-in of God's kingdom, in Revelation the end-time rise of the beast and his overthrow are understood as *results* of that initial breaking-in, that *parousia* which is the Lord's "coming" (Mt. 24:27), indeed the *apocalyptein*, the apocalypse of Jesus Christ (1 Cor. 1:7; Rev. 1:1). The "mystery" (knowledge previously hidden but now revealed, Rom. 16:25-26) of the second coming referred to by Paul (1 Cor. 15:51; Eph. 1:9-10) and in John's vision (Rev. 10:7) appears to be precisely this: what Daniel is commanded to seal—that is, the time relationship between the rule and ultimate destruction of the beast-king and the coming of Messiah the prince (Dan.

11:21-24, 36-38, 45; 12:1-4)—John is commanded to reveal: rather than necessarily *following* events predicted by Daniel, the coming of the Lord *initiates* events which include a blasphemous beast-ruler whose true character will be revealed after three and one half years (Rev. 13:1-8) and who will dominate the earth for a like period until Christ returns to earth with his saints to destroy him (Rev. 19:11-21; cf. 1 Thess. 4:15-18; 2 Thess. 2:8-12).

Revelation's use of some of Daniel's imagery and phraseology, then, should not mislead the reader into interpreting both books as historical apocalyptic; as I have argued earlier in these pages, Daniel is indeed historical apocalyptic, but Revelation is eschatological apocalyptic, insisting again and again in explicit statement, visionary imagery, and literary structure that believers must look expectantly for Christ's revelation, his second advent into the world, to occur at any moment.

It is as though one central motivation guided John in composing his book: to support the admonitions of Jesus in the Gospels and of the apostles in their letters to the churches to be constantly on the watch for his return and the inauguration of God's kingdom "in earth as it is in heaven" (Mt. 6:10; representative texts include Mt. 24:42, 25:13; Mk. 13:35; Lk. 12:45, 21:36; 1 Cor. 1:7, 15:23; 1 Thess. 4:15; Jas. 5:8; 2 Pet. 3:4ff.). Between Christ's resurrection and his ascension, when the apostles pressed him to reveal the time when God's kingdom should appear (though their primary interest was not so much in the heavenly kingdom coming to earth as in the restoration of earthly kingdom status to Israel), Jesus reiterated what he had taught them already: only God the Father controls the timing of events and his schedule is not for human beings to know (Acts 1:6-7; cf. Mk. 13:32, Mt. 24:36).

But while Revelation assumes no necessary historical circumstances nor any previously obligatory fulfillment of prophecy to precede the appearance of Jesus and the breaking into time of eternal reality, once that initial event occurs there is a necessary unfolding of future developments within a short period of

time. Revelation uses phrases and imagery from Daniel to delineate this brief
interval between the second advent of Christ and the establishment on earth of
God's heavenly kingdom. These include the "time, times, and a half" (Dan.
7:25,12:7; Rev. 12:14); the beast from the sea (Dan. 7:3; Rev. 13:1—four beasts
rise from the sea in Daniel, whereas one rises from the sea and one from the earth
in Revelation; both Daniel's and Revelation's beasts from the sea have ten horns,
and the bestial descriptions are similar, Dan. 7:4-8 with Rev. 13:1-3); and a period
of twelve hundred plus days, 1260 days or forty-two months in Revelation
(11:2,12:6,13:5) and 1290 in Daniel (12:11, adjusted to 1335 days in 12:12).

Since the number of days equates roughly with three and one-half years,
the "time, times, and a half" of both Daniel (12:7, 7:25) and Revelation (12:14)
apparently specify a time-limit to the most vicious depredations of a beast-ruler,
portrayed in Daniel's dream as a "little horn" (Dan. 7:8, 8:9) sprung from the
fourth and most terrible of the rulers of the vision (Dan. 7:3-7) and in Revelation
as a beast from the sea empowered by Satan to rule the world with the aid of
"another beast" from the earth (Rev. 13:1-5, 11-15). In Daniel this powerful ruler
prevails against "the saints of the Most High [for] a time, and times, and the
dividing of time" and then his kingdom is consumed and replaced by God's
"everlasting kingdom" (Dan. 7:25-27; cf. 2:44-45). In Revelation the beast-ruler
wars against and overcomes the saints and prevails for forty-two months (Rev.
13:5-6); during this same period of time two prophet-martyrs with supernatural
power testify against the beast, and though they are killed at the end of the time,
they are resurrected and called up to heaven (Rev. 11:3-12) in language
reminiscent both of John's translation to heaven (Rev. 4:1) and Christ's ascension
(Acts 1:9). In a vision between that of the two martyrs and that of the rise of the
beasts John sees "a woman clothed with the sun" who brings forth a "child to
rule all nations with a rod of iron" and is divinely protected from the attempts of
the dragon-serpent (the power behind the beast-ruler) to destroy her and her child
(Rev. 12:1,5-6,13-16). Although the woman's child is destined to "rule all nations

with a rod of iron,'' that he is "caught up unto God, and to his throne" when the dragon attempts to devour him (Rev. 12:4-5, cf. 19:15) indicates that this vision encompasses not only the coming reign of Christ but also his past incarnation, death, resurrection, and ascension; since the vision seems to combine salvation history and prophecy using the same symbols, the scene serves as a warning against too quickly assuming that others of the book's series of visions are presented chronologically. Indeed, this vision reverts to eternal pre-history in its description of the "war in heaven" and Satan's fall (Rev. 12:7-9), though its description of the woman's divine protection from the dragon is placed within the "time, and times, and half a time" of the beast's most savage rule (Rev. 12:14-16).

In order to parallel him with Revelation's "mighty angel" with the open book (Rev. 10:1-2), who swears that the "mystery of God [will soon] be finished" (Rev. 10:5-7), we now return to the "man clothed in linen," who swears that the end of Daniel's beast-king will come within "a time, times, and a half" (Dan. 12:7). These similar divine figures appearing in both Daniel and Revelation with their distinctive proclamations may help clarify in iconographic as well as verbal terms the distinction I am making between the two apocalypses. The similarities between Daniel's man in linen and Revelation's risen Christ have been discussed briefly above (p. 107). What remains is to point out the parallels between the two divine figures, suggest their identity, and note the differences in their actions and words.

The figure in Daniel is girdled with gold, his face is like lightning, his eyes like lamps of fire, his arms and feet have the appearance of polished brass, and his voice resounds like the combined voices of a multitude (Dan. 10:5-6). In his second appearance, he stands upon the river Hiddekel, holds up both hands to heaven, and swears by the Eternal that the "end of these wonders" (12:6) will be "for a time, times, and a half; and when he shall have accomplished to scatter the power of the holy people, all these things shall be finished" (Dan. 12:7). The figure in Revelation has a rainbow upon his head, his face shines like the sun, and his feet are like pillars of fire. With a "little book open" in his right hand, he sets his right foot on the sea and his left on the earth, lifts his hand to heaven, and swears by the Eternal Creator that "there shall be time no longer" (Rev. 10:1-6; the oath is better translated "There shall be no more delay," 10:6, NEB); he concludes, "in the days of the voice of the seventh angel, when he shall begin to sound [his trumpet], the mystery of God [shall] be finished" as prophesied (10:7). Both figures share features in common with the risen Christ as envisioned by John (Rev. 1:13-16); the following tabulation indicates the extent to which the figures in Daniel and in Revelation share characteristics of the glorified Christ in John's inaugural vision. The chart also shows one feature shared by the figures in Revelation 1 and 10 which is not present in Daniel.

Christ in Prologue	Man in Linen	Mighty Angel
Rev. 1:10-11, 13-16	Dan. 10:5-6,18-19; 12:6-7	Rev. 10:1-11
voice of trumpet	voice of multitude	voice of lion
body-length garment	clothed in linen	clothed with cloud
feet of brass	arms/feet of brass	feet of fire
orders writing	shows truth for writing	orders prophecy
touches prophet	touches prophet	gives prophet book
golden girdle	golden girdle	
"fear not"	"fear not"	
eyes of fire	eyes of fire	
face like sun	[face like lightning]	face like sun
	oath w/lifted hands	oath w/lifted hand
	stands on river	stands on sea/earth
	"seal the book"	"seal 7 thunders"

As shown above, five characteristics are shared by all three of the figures from Daniel and Revelation, three characteristics are shared by the figures in Revelation 1 and in Daniel 10-12, three by the figures in Revelation 10 and in Daniel 10-12, and one common feature of the figures in Revelation 1 and 10 does not appear in Daniel 10-12 (though in all three figures, the brilliance of the face is emphasized). Therefore, the imagistic evidence for identifying the "mighty angel" of Revelation 10 with the risen Lord of the churches in Revelation 1 is overwhelming; furthermore, it hardly seems open to doubt that the author of Revelation uses Danielic imagery from Daniel 10 and 12 not only to delineate the figure of Jesus Christ in his book but also to suggest that the "man in linen" of Daniel's vision is a pre-incarnate form of the Son of God. That this figure is to be regarded as indeed more than an angel is already implied in the Book of Daniel by the marked contrast between his appearances and those of Gabriel, an angel who delivers information to the prophet on two occasions (Dan. 8:16, 9:21) but as a sent messenger and with none of the extraordinarily arresting visual description that distinguishes the "man in linen."

As shown by the analysis above, some actions and words of the divine figure in Daniel are the same as or quite similar to those of the Christ-figure in Revelation: both touch the prophet, tell him not to fear, give him information to communicate or to seal, take up an unusually dramatic stance, raise hands to swear an oath. However, the interaction between divine person and human prophet is quite different. In Daniel the prophet, weakened by a three-week fast, is first addressed by an angel, then by the one who has the "appearance of a man"; since Daniel must be first strengthened and encouraged by the touch and words of both an angel and the man, only then can he look, listen, and report clearly the divine narration, though he still does not understand its full significance nor the time of its fulfillment (10:18-12:13). In Revelation, although John suffers no collapse and hears undismayed the voices of the "mighty angel" and of the seven thunders and immediately begins to write, he does not distinguish the words of the angel and he is forbidden by another "voice from heaven" to write the utterance of the seven thunders (10:3-4). Yet John expresses no difficulty in understanding the oath sworn by the mighty angel that God's judgment shall no longer be delayed upon the sounding of the seventh trumpet, whereas Daniel does not understand the cryptic oath of the man in linen and, instead of receiving an explanation, he is told to seal the words until "the time of the end" and is dismissed with "Go thy way, Daniel" (Rev. 10:5-7; Dan. 12:7-9,13). The similarities and differences between the oath scenes in Daniel and Revelation firmly connect those scenes visually while distinguishing between the central message to the prophet in each scene. The message to Daniel is sealed to await further historical developments over an indefinite period of time; the message to John is open, though its reception has both bitter and sweet consequences. The combined resonance of the two oath scenes suggests that the latter reveals the meaning of the former: the "time, times, and a half" during which the beast-ruler will be destroyed and God's everlasting kingdom established, once initiated by the coming of Christ, will not be delayed but will move swiftly toward the final union of heaven and earth.

The contrast between bitter and sweet in the message to Daniel, though not made explicit, is implied in the severely brutish and blasphemous rule of the "vile person" (Dan. 11:21) on the one hand and the ultimate victory of God on behalf of those "found written in the book" (Dan. 12:1) on the other; in Revelation the bitter and the sweet of God's judgments upon the evil of the world and his making all things new in eternity are made explicit through the image of the book John ingests and its resulting sweet taste in the mouth and nauseating effects in the stomach (10:9-10; cf. Ezek. 2:8-3:3). The angel's following statement, "Thou must prophesy again before many peoples, and nations, and tongues, and kings" (10:11), anticipates the continuing effect of John's book throughout the future.

The fulfillment of the promised blessings on those who have studied and sought to understand his prophetic book (1:3; 22:7) and its pleasure can be measured by the great volume of commentary and criticism the book has generated; on the other hand, the frustration, confusion, and even pain the book's visions of divine vengeance have caused some readers are evident in that same body of commentary. We have seen some examples. D. H. Lawrence moved beyond his strong distaste to a kind of transcendentalist toleration of the book as mystical poetry, but he remarked that as a chapel-going child, the Apocalypse "always aroused in [him] a real dislike"; it was, he said, and to some extent remained for him in adulthood, "the most detestable of all [the] books of the Bible" (61). And John Hersey speaks of Revelation as a "strange book [representing] a total negation of the hopeful words of the Gospels. . .[it] dismays me" (355). On the other side, George Eliot was enthralled by Revelation, and its imaginative structure and symbolism inform several of her novels, particularly *Romola*, mentioned earlier. Set in fifteenth-century Florence, the novel offers Eliot's answers to "the crucial question of the prophet's authenticity" as it reinterprets and applies in fiction the patterns and symbols of the Apocalypse (Carpenter and Landow 303).

To return to the oath scenes, their placement within the overall structure of the Book of Daniel and the Book of Revelation indicates the relative importance of each to its context and, in the case of Revelation, the importance of its relationship to its mirror scene in Daniel. The scene in Daniel occurs at the very end of the book, while the scene in Revelation is placed near the book's center. Instead of concluding, as in Daniel, a series of six narratives and four apocalyptic visions, all emphasizing the illusory nature of human kingdoms in time against the background of the reality of God's sovereign rule through eternity, with an enigmatic and mysterious prophecy of a divinely appointed yet historically dependent end, an *eschata*, Revelation places in the middle of a series of letters to churches and apocalyptic visions, all emphasizing the imminence of the *eschata* as an incentive to steadfastness in "the word of God and . . . the testimony of Jesus Christ," a central vision of God's taking his sovereign initiative to judge and make new the universe in accord with prophecies he has revealed and to do so with no delay occasioned by human actions.

Perhaps the most telling images to intensify the contrast between Daniel's and Revelation's oath scenes are the sealed book and the open book. The only sealed book in Revelation is opened early by the worthy Lamb (5:1-6:1) and among the last commands to John is "Seal not . . . this book" (22:10). As we have seen, the only sealing required of John conceals from his readers what the seven thunders said (10:4), but lack of their content does not affect the revelation of the *eschata*, which is fully declared (10:7).

The positioning of these oath scenes is appropriate to the outlook of each book: Daniel proceeds primarily in a linear, chronological line from the fall of Jerusalem to the reign of Cyrus (the exception is the flashback of Chapters 7 and 8) with an announcement of the time of the end coming at the end of the book; Revelation moves cyclically with the prologue and epilogue mirroring each other, the intra-textual allusions in the letters to the churches pointing both back to the prologue and ahead to the new Jerusalem, and each of the sevens in the series of apocalyptic visions essentially repeating in differing imagery the cataclysmic judgments to fall upon the earth before the godless are destroyed and the heavens and the earth are made new as a home for God and his people. In Revelation the announcement of the accomplishment of the *eschata* without longer delay comes to the prophet between the sixth and seventh trumpets, *in medias res*, as it were, himself already elevated to the perspective of the throne of God and therefore a symbol of those to be caught up at the imminent coming of Christ; the scene intervenes as well between apocalyptic visions of terrible woes on earth and a foreview of the victory of God and his saints in the vision of the two resurrected martyrs who ascend to heaven in the sight of their enemies. Thus the eschatological outlook of Revelation, the importance of the upward, expectant look in the midst of trials and persecutions, is reflected in its structure: all radiates outward and backward and forward from a center. The outlook is not that of

Daniel, which is to peer forward anxiously toward a distant horizon of the future, with faith in God's ultimate victory, of course, but conscious of the necessity to suffer through the painfully slow movement of history toward that longed-for goal and of the probability of a long sleep in the dust before that day (Dan. 12:2). The outlook of Revelation encompasses that view as well, for centuries have already passed since Christ's promise to return and many more may pass yet; but Revelation urges each individual Christian, each generation, to maintain the enthusiastic expectation of first-century Christianity: in Pauline terms, to "live soberly, righteously, and godly, in this present world; looking for that blessed hope, and the glorious appearing of the great God and our Saviour Jesus Christ" (Titus 2:12-13).

There are many ways of describing the structure of Revelation. I list a few of those most interesting to me. In a series of articles Kenneth Strand divides the book into an overall chiastic pattern of eight prophetic sequences, further divided into two sets of four with the center between Chapters 14 and 15; the first four are "historical," the last four "eschatological-judgment" visions (*AUSS* 25-28). Adela Collins also divides Revelation into "two great halves" *(Combat Myth* 20-21), but in her scheme the watershed occurs between Chapters 11 and 12, with each half encompassing three series of sevens and Chapter 12 serving as a paradigm for the whole book because of its combat myth structure. Finally Elisabeth Fiorenza's structure for Revelation is the closest in form to mine of those I have seen. She describes a seven-part structure and designates the parts as A B C D C' B' A'. She supports the pattern as one familiar to John's audience: identically balanced structures appeared on images engraved on Roman coins of A. D. 35-36 and in the golden candelabra sculpted on the Arch of Titus in Rome.[20] She comments: "In choosing [this] concentric pattern [A B C D C' B' A'] the author [John] makes the small scroll of prophecy in Rev. 10:1-15:4 the climactic center of the action [in a work intended as] prophecy in the form of the apostolic letter" *(Justice* 176-177). In my own drawing of Revelation's structure on page 119 I include Fiorenza's chiastic designations and indicate her differing chapter and verse references for the seven parts.

In the figure which follows I attempt to bring together in one diagram a representation of all my previous comments about the structure of Revelation: interlocking sections, mirroring units, intra-textual allusions that point backward or forward, and a radiating center. The diagram as pictured is seen from the top; seen from the side, the illustration would have the appearance of ascending and descending stairs with 10:1-14:20 as the highest point joining the two sets of stairs. The broken lines connecting the prologue and epilogue with the sections adjacent to each represent the deliberate repetitions of word and image which anchor each end to the whole. All the divisions, seen from the side as a whole, can be given the look of the *menorah*, as Payne does, although he uses different references for the divisions (370) and his figure includes no raised center.

Repeated here as well is a drawing of the structure suggested in Part I for Daniel, showing its chiastic structure in Chapters 2-7 (the Aramaic section) and the interconnecting themes and images that tie both the Hebrew and Aramaic segments and the narrative and visionary halves together.[21] The way certain narratives in Daniel anticipate imagery and theme in the visions and are in turn echoed by the visions is similar to Revelation's anticipations of later visions in the prologue and letters section and the corresponding echoes near the end of the book.

The Structure of Revelation

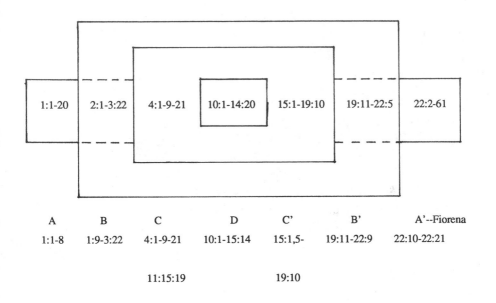

A	B	C	D	C'	B'	A'--Fiorena
1:1-8	1:9-3:22	4:1-9-21	10:1-15:14	15:1,5-	19:11-22:9	22:10-22:21
		11:15:19		19:10		

The Structure of Daniel

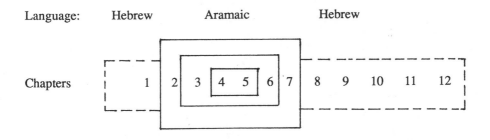

NOTES TO REVELATION
AND "SHAPE AS MEANING"

[1]For an excellently focused review of scholarship on Revelation of the past five and one-half decades, see Fiorenza, *Justice*, 12-32.

[2]Barr, "Reader" 84, admitting being "overly attentive [counts] seven levels of narration," but his placement of John between God and the readers (the seven churches) corresponds to mine.

[3]Güttgemanns argues, in a complex study seeking to relate John's visions to Freudian dream theory as well as to the grammatology of Derrida and the "phantastic literature" described by Todorov, that the "Son of Man" is actually the metonym of John's repressed desire for universal dominion to replace that exercised by the godless powers. The process by which the transference is accomplished is the writing on earth of a book which is effectively rewritten as a palimpsest of a celestial original revealed in a dream. "In der Metonymie des 'Menschensohns' ereignet sich die 'Wiederkehr des Verdrängten'" (49).

[4]Aune 195 emphasizes that the seven letters to the churches, "unlike the epistolary framework . . ., betray no single feature of the Pauline or early Christian epistolary tradition."

[5]For a brief review of the hesitation among some early Christians to accept and use the Apocalypse, see Mackay 223-225. Coyle 14-17 points out that, although Augustine includes Revelation in his A. D. 396 listing of canonical books, he gives the book only belated and limited attention in his writings.

⁶For the major alternatives and their attendant problems see Collins, "Dating," 33-45.

⁷Elsewhere, Fiorenza locates the center more broadly as 10:1-15:4 (175). There are, of course, different methods of calculating the exact center of the book. If one uses the number of verses in the KJV, one finds the center at 12:7, the "war in heaven," since 201 verses both precede and follow 12:7. This event is traditionally placed in distant pre-history, even pre-creation as in Milton's *Paradise Lost*, "The Argument," Book I, Hughes 211.

⁸Miller 10-16 reviews classical uses of the word *chilias* to mean, e. g., "number beyond computation" and "so many as to be incalculable," thus seeming to oppose the belief in a literal thousand-year reign of Christ. His main point turns out to be, however, that the literalism of *chiliasm* can paradoxically be trans-personalized into a freedom to imagine and act in the face of apocalyptic closure (21-22). Although I read Chapter 20 as presenting a literal millennial reign of Christ, the textual arguments against the view marshalled by R. Fowler White *passim* are impressive.

⁹This outline would require much further subdividing to accommodate the many shifts of emphasis, interludes, interrupting scenes, apostrophes, and parentheses which occur throughout, but particularly in the sections designated "Apocalypse." This outline, however, should clarify the larger, interlocking movements of the work and, therefore, its dominant theme: *the imminent bursting into time of the reality of God's eternal kingdom with the concomitant destruction of the illusory strength of anti-God forces and the resulting eternal union of God with his people*. The Apocalypse as revealed to John is essentially the dazzling incarnation into dramatic poetry of Daniel's proto-typical figures: the great image of successive vainglorious earthly powers smashed to nothingness by "a stone cut out without hands" which burgeons into a worldwide, eternal kingdom (Dan. 2:31-35) and the apparently invincible ultimate beast-ruler of the world who shall

suddenly come "to his end and none shall help him" after which the "wise shall shine as the brightness of the firmament" (Dan. 11:45-12:3).

[10]Barr 55-57 correlates the oral rhetoric of Revelation with "a social situation of cultural anomie" in which the original audience found itself. Yet he states, albeit parenthetically, that that audience's experiences are "common to most Christians and most places," thus implying that the book has a universal applicability and a timeless relevance.

[11]Bowman 23-25 says of the arrangement I call an elongated oval, "the seven churches [are] arranged in the form of the seven-branched candlestick of the Herodian Temple—Nos. 1 and 7, 2 and 6, 3 and 5 forming pairs on opposite sides with No. 4 at the top. . .[;] *seven churches* signifies the Church Universal" (italics his).

[12]Minear 58 notes the "significant variant in the location" of the command to hear, but assumes the same function for it throughout the letters. Wendland 376 graphically displays the seven common features of the seven letters but does not comment on the shift in the order of promise and exhortation to hear. He does identify churches 2 and 6 as significantly different from the other five in receiving not condemnation but commendation. To his impressive list of sevens in Revelation should be added Rushdoony's "seven beatitudes": 1:3, 14:13, 16:15, 19:9, 20:6, 22:7, and 22:14.

[13]Enroth observes that the "hearing formula," repeated seven times in 2-3, is again repeated in 13:9 and that all eight uses are also connected verbally with 1:3: "hear the words of this prophecy." She further notes that 13:9 occurs "in the middle of chapters 12-14," thus looking backward toward the beast from the sea (13:1-8) and forward to the beast from the earth (13:11-18), the ultimate victory of the saints (14:1-5), and the judgment of the evil rulers (14:17-20). Enroth 608 interprets these occurrences in their contexts as neither threats of judgment nor signals to understand a mystery, but as "an encouragement [underlying] the promise and the possibility of salvation."

[14]Minear follows Koester, "Lamm und Kirche in der Apokalypse," *Vom Wort des Lebens*, ed. M. Meinertz (Münster, 1951), 157.

[15]Wendland 378 designates as "Interludes" the parallel interruptions between the sixth and seventh seals and the sixth and seventh trumpets. Both are reassurances to the faithful "consistent with the [essentially optimistic] theme and purpose of Revelation." His highly detailed and annotated outline is helpful for the reader, though somewhat overly homiletical.

[16]Wendland 380-381 incorporates these seven figures into a broader group of "seven signs," stretching from 11:19 to 15:4, thus unnecessarily merging diverse segments of the whole.

[17]See Böcher 169 for a fascinating drawing of the heavenly Jerusalem, combining biblical and astrological signs and featuring God the Father and Son at the city's center imaged as sun and moon.

[18]Minear 61 identifies in 21:8, the list of disobedient rebels banished from the Holy City, echoes from the letters to the seven cities of Asia: "the cowards (2:10,13), the disloyal (2:10,13), the fornicators (2:14,20), the idolaters (2:14,20), and . . . the liars (deceivers and deceived) (2:2,9,20; 3:9)."

[19]Sneen 116-117 outlines the common elements shared by the apocalyptic teaching of Jesus in Mark, Matthew, and Luke with the Apocalypse of John. Casey 42 sees John's use of the Exodus from Egypt as a type of redemption, judgment, and inheritance as distinguishing Revelation from other New Testament books, citing e.g., 1 Cor. 5:7, 10:1-11; Rom. 3:24; 2 Pet. 2:5, 9-10; John 6. "For John [in Revelation] the Exodus is the event which orders and gives shape to his hope" and a reenactment of an Exodus-like redemption of God's people, judgment of their oppressors, and entry into full inheritance is "what must soon take place, Rev. 22:6."

[20]Payne 367-371 includes a photograph of the candlestick on the Arch of Titus and a drawing of the menorah as the "possible structure" of Revelation: for him the center candle represents Rev. 11:1-14:20.

[21]Steven Thompson 106-107 concludes that there are "very close links to *biblical* Hebrew/Aramaic [italics his]" in the syntactical structures of the Greek of Revelation; "a few syntactical constructions . . . are far more at home in Aramaic than in OT Hebrew." His study tempts one to see another parallel between Daniel and Revelation, the involvement at some stage of two languages. Thompson cautiously urges reconsideration of the extremes in scholarship—i.e., the insistence that Hebrew only or Aramaic exclusively underlies the Greek text: it is "safest to assume that . . . the primary source of Semitic influence . . . is biblical Hebrew, and biblical Aramaic."

WORKS CITED ON REVELATION
AND "SHAPE AS MEANING"

Aune, D. E. "The Form and Function of the Proclamations to the Seven Churches (Revelation 2-3)." *New Testament Studies*, 36 (1990): 182-204.

Barr, David L. "How Were the Hearers Blessed? Literary Reflections on the Social Impact of John's Apocalypse." *Proceedings of the Eastern Great Lakes and Midwest Bible Society*. Ed. P. Reditt. 8 (1988): 49-59.

_____. The Reader of/in the Apocalypse: Exploring a Method." *Proceedings of the Eastern Great Lakes and Midwest Bible Society*. Ed. T. Callan. 10 (1990): 79-91.

Beale, G. K. *The Use of Daniel in Jewish Apocalyptic Literature and in the Revelation of St. John*. Lanham, Md.: University P of America, 1984.

Bell, Albert A. "The Date of John's Apocalypse: The Evidence of Some Roman Historians Reconsidered." *New Testament Studies*, 25 (October 1978): 1:93-102.

Böcher, Otto. "Mythos und Rationalität in der Apokalypse der Johannes." *Mythos and Rationalität*. Hrsg. Hans Heinrich Schmid. Gütersloh: Gütersloher Verlagshaus Mohn, 1988. 163-171.

Bodinger, Martin. "Le Mythe de Néron de L'Apocalypse de Saint Jean au Talmud de Babylone." *Revue de l'Histoire des Religions*, 206 (1989), 1:21-40.

Bowman, John Wick. *The Drama of Revelation: An Account of the Book with a New Translation in the Language of Today*. Philadelphia: Westminster P, 1955.

Buber, Martin. "Prophecy, Apocalyptic, and the Historical Hour." *On the Bible: Eighteen Studies by Martin Buber*. Ed. Nahum N. Glatzer. New York: Schocken Books, 1968.

Carpenter, Mary Wilson and George P. Landow. "Ambiguous Revelations: the Apocalypse and Victorian Literature." *The Apocalypse in English Renaissance Thought and Literature*. See Patrides and Wittreich below. 299-322.

Casey, Jay. "The Exodus Theme in the Book of Revelation Against the Background of the New Testament." *Exodus—A Lasting Paradigm*. Ed. Bas van Iersel and Anton Weiler. Edinburgh: T. & T. Clark, 1987. A special edition of *Concilium: Religion in the Eighties*, No. 189 (Feb. 1987). 34-43.

Collins, Adela Yarbro. *The Combat Myth in the Book of Revelation*. Missoula, MT: Scholars P, 1976.

_____. *Crisis and Catharsis: The Power of the Apocalypse*. Philadelphia: Westminster P, 1984.

_____. "Dating the Apocalypse of John," *Biblical Research Review*, 26 (1981): 33-45.

_____. Persecution and Vengeance in the Book of Revelation." *Apocalypticism in the Mediterranean World and the Near East. Proceedings of the International Colloquium on Apocalypticism, Uppsala, August 12-17, 1979*. Second Edition. Ed. David Hellholm. Tübingen: J. C. B. Mohr (Paul Siebeck), 1989. 729-749.

Court, John M. *Myth and History in the Book of Revelation*. Atlanta: John Knox P, 1979.

Coyle, J. Kevin. "Augustine and Apocalyptic: Thoughts on the Fall of Rome, The Book of Revelation, and the End of the World." *Florilegium: Carleton University Annual Papers on Late Antiquity and the Middle Ages*, 9 (1987): 1-34.

Derrida, Jacques. "On an Apocalyptic Tone Recently Adopted in Philosophy." From *Les fins de l'homme*. Paris: Editions Galilee, 1982. Translated by John P. Leavy in *Semeia* 23 (1982): 63-97, and quoted in Cleo McNelly Kearns, "Apocalypse and Wisdom," *Christianity and Literature*, 41 (Winter 1992): 121-139.

Efird, James M. *Daniel and Revelation: A Study of Two Extraordinary Visions*. Valley Forge: Judson P, 1978.

Enroth, Anne Marit. "The Hearing Formula in the Book of Revelation." *New Testament Studies*, 36 (1990): 598-608.

Field, Rosalind. "The Heavenly Jerusalem in *Pearl*." *The Modern Language Review*, 81 (1987): 7-17.

Fiorenza, Elisabeth Schüssler. *The Book of Revelation: Justice and Judgment*. Philadelphia: Fortress P, 1985.

_____. "Revelation." *The New Testament and its Modern Interpreters*. Eds. Eldon J. Epp and George W. MacRae. Philadelphia: Fortress P, 1989. 407-427.

_____. *Revelation: A Vision of a Just World*. Minneapolis: Fortress P, 1991.

Fitts, William David. "*Cymbeline* and The Woman in the Wilderness: The Twelfth Chapter of the Apocalypse as a Source Study." Unpublished dissertation, Texas A&M University, 1985.

Fowler, Alastair. A *History of English Literature*. Cambridge: Harvard UP, 1987.

Freyne, Seán. "Reading Hebrews and Revelation Intertextually." *Intertextuality in Biblical Writings: Essays in Honour of Bas van Iersel*. Ed. Sipke Draisma. Omslag Henk Biekkenhorst[?]: Uitgeversmaatschappij J.H. Kok-Kampen, 1989. 83-93.

Guthrie, Donald. *The Relevance of John's Apocalypse*. Grand Rapids: Eerdmans, 1987.

Güttgemanns, Erhardt. "Die Semiotik des Traums in apokalyptischen Texten am Beispiel von Apokalypse Johannis I." *Linguistica Biblica: Interdisziplinare Zeitschrift für Theologie und Linguistik*, 59 (1987): 7-54.

Hassel, R. Chris Jr. "Last Words and Last Things: St. John, Apocalypse, and Eschatology in *Richard III*." *Shakespeare Studies*, 18 (1986): 25-40.

Hellholm, David. "The Visions He Saw Or: To Encode the Future in Writing: An Analysis of the Prologue of John's Apocalyptic Letter." *Text and Logos: The Humanistic Interpretation of the New Testament*. Ed. Theodore W. Jennings, Jr. Atlanta: Scholars P, 1990. 109-146.

Hemer, Colin J. *The Letters to the Seven Churches of Asia in Their Local Setting*. Sheffield: JSOT, 1986.

Hersey, John. "The Revelation of Saint John the Divine." *Incarnation: Contemporary Writers on the New Testament*. Ed. Alfred Corn. Viking Penguin, 1990. 346-355.

Hughes, Merritt Y., Ed. *John Milton: Complete Poems and Major Prose*. New York: Odyssey P, 1957.

Jenkins, R. B. "Revelation in *Paradise Regained*." *Journal of Evolutionary Psychology*, 6 (1985): 269-283.

Keller, Catherine. "Die Frau in der Wüste: ein feministisch-theologischer Midrasch zu Offb 12." *Evangelische Theologische*, 50 (1990), 5:414-432.

Kessler, Edward. *Flannery O'Connor and the Language of Apocalypse*. Princeton: Princeton UP, 1986.

Kirby, John T. "The Rhetorical Situation of Revelation 1-3." *New Testament Studies*, 34 (1988): 197-207.

Kraft, Heinrich. *Die Offenbarung des Johannes. Handbuch zum Neuen Testament*, 16a. Tübingen: JCB Mohr (Paul Siebeck), 1974.

Lawrence, D. H. *Apocalypse and the Writings on Revelation*. Ed. Mara Kalnins. Cambridge: Cambridge UP, 1980.

Mackay, Thomas W. "Early Christian Millenarianist Interpretation of the Two Witnesses in John's Apocalypse 11:3-13." *By Study and Also By Faith*. Ed. John M. Lundquist and Stephen D. Ricks. Salt Lake City: Deseret Book Co., 1990. 222-331.

McGinn, Bernard. "Early Apocalypticism: The Ongoing Debate." *The Apocalypse in English Renaissance Thought and Literature*. See Patrides and Wittreich below. 2-39.

———. "Revelation." *The Literary Guide to the Bible*. Eds. Robert Alter and Frank Kermode. The Belknap P of Harvard UP, 1987. 523-541.

Meyer, Jerry. "The Woman Clothed With the Sun: Two Illustrations to St. John's Revelation by William Blake." *Studies in Iconography*, 12 (1988): 148-160.

Michaels, J. Ramsey. "Jewish and Christian Apocalyptic Letters: 1 Peter, Revelation, and 2 Baruch 78-87." *SBL Seminar Papers*, 26 (1987): 268-275.

Mickelson, A. Berkeley. *Daniel and Revelation: Riddles or Realities?* Nashville: T. Nelson, 1984.

Miller, David. "Chiliasm: Apocalyptic with a Thousand Faces." *Facing Apocalypse*. Ed. Valerie Andrews, Robert Bosnak, and Karen Walter Goodwin. Dallas: Spring Publications, Inc., 1987. 5-24.

Minear, Paul S. *I Saw a New Earth: An Introduction to the Visions of the Apocalypse*. Washington: Corpus Books, 1968.

Patrides, C. A., and Joseph Wittreich, eds. *The Apocalypse in English Renaissance Thought and Literature: Patterns, Antecedents, and Repercussions*. Ithaca: Cornell UP, 1984.

_____. " 'Something Like Prophetick Strain': Apocalyptic Configurations in Milton.'' *The Apocalypse in English Renaissance Thought and Literature.* See Patrides and Wittreich above. 207-237.

Paulien, Jon. "Elusive Allusions: The Problematic Use of the Old Testament in Revelation." *Biblical Research.* 33 (1988): 37-53.

Payne, Michael. "Voice, Metaphor, and Narrative in the Book of Revelation." *Mappings of the Biblical Terrain: The Bible as Text.* Ed. Vincent L. Tollers and John Maier. Lewisburg: Bucknell UP, 1990. 364-372.

Perisho, Steve. "The Structure of Flannery O'Connor's 'Revelation'." *Notes on Contemporary Literature,* 20 (1990) 4:5-7.

Priest, James E. "Contemporary Apocalyptic Scholarship and the Revelation." *Johannine Studies: Essays in Honor of Frank Pack.* Ed. James E. Priest. Malibu: Pepperdine University Press, 1989. 182-204.

Pritchard, John Paul. *A Literary Approach to the New Testament.* Norman: U of Oklahoma P, 1975.

Robinson, John Arthur Thomas. *Redating the New Testament.* Philadelphia: Westminster P, 1976.

Roloff, Jürgen. "'Siehe, ich stehe vor der Tür und klopfe an': Beobachtungen zur überlieferungsgeschichte von Offb. 3,20." *In Vom Ürchristentum zu Jesus: Für Joachim Gnilka.* Hrsg. Hubert Frankemoelle und Karl Kertelge. Freiburg: Herder, 1989. 452-466.

Rushdoony, Rousas John. *Thy Kingdom Come: Studies in Daniel and Revelation.* Nutley, NJ: Presbyterian and Reformed, 1971.

Schneiders, Sandra M. *The Revelatory Text: Interpreting the New Testament as Sacred Scripture.* Harper: San Francisco, 1991.

Smalley, Stephen S. "John's Revelation and John's Community." *Bulletin of the John Rylands Library,* 69 (Spring 1987): 549-571.

Sneen, Donald. *Visions of Hope.* Minneapolis: Augsburg P, 1978.

Strand, Kenneth A. "The Eight Basic Visions in the Book of Revelation." *Andrews University Seminary Studies*, 25 (Spring 1987): 107-121.

_____. " 'Overcomers': A Study in the Macrodynamics of Theme Development in the Book of Revelation." *AUSS*, 28 (Autumn 1990): 237-254.

_____. "The 'Spotlight on Last Events' Sections in the Book of Revelation." *AUSS*, 27 (Autumn 1989): 201-221.

_____. "The 'Victorious-Introduction' Scenes in the Visions of the Book of Revelation." *AUSS*, 25 (Autumn 1987): 267-288.

Thompson, Leonard L. "The Literary Unity of the Book of Revelation." *Mappings of the Biblical Terrain: The Bible as Text*. Eds. Vincent L. Tollers and John Maier. Lewisburg: Bucknell UP, 1990. 347-363.

Thompson, Steven. *The Apocalypse and Semitic Syntax*. Cambridge: Cambridge UP, 1985.

Wendland, Ernst R. "7 X 7 (X7): A Structural and Thematic Outline of John's Apocalypse." *OPTAT*, 4 (1990): 371-386.

White, John L. "The Structural Analysis of Philemon: A Point of Departure in the Formal Analysis of the Pauline Letter." *The Society of Biblical Literature 107th Annual Meeting Seminar Papers (28-31 October 1971)*. Atlanta, 1971. Vol. 1:1-48.

White, R. Fowler. "Reexamining the Evidence for Recaptulation in Rev. 20:1-10." *Wesleyan Theological Journal*, 51 (1989): 319-344.

Willis, John T. "The Old Testament and the Book of Revelation." *Johannine Studies: Essays in Honor of Frank Pack*. Ed. James E. Priest. Malibu: Pepperdine UP, 1989. 231-239.

Wittreich, Joseph. "'Image of that Horror': The Apocalypse in *King Lear*." *The Apocalypse in English Renaissance Thought and Literature*. See Patrides and Wittreich above. 175-206.

PART IV

We shall not cease from exploration
And the end of all our exploring
Will be to arrive where we started
And know the place for the first time.
—T. S. Eliot

Chapter 9

Personal Afterword

Soon after returning from the Pacific at the close of World War II, I entered the university and began studies intended to prepare me for a theological seminary and then life as a Christian minister. While an undergraduate I was first licensed by my church and later ordained to preach the Gospel of Christ and fulfill the role of pastor. My first sermon was on the letter to the church at Ephesus in the Book of Revelation. My choice of a text from the Apocalypse reflected a fascination that had begun when, as a boy beginning to read whole books, I had attempted time after time, without much success, to understand what Revelation is about. Although then I could discern no logical progression of thought nor grasp rationally a coherent plot, I had luxuriated in the amazingly vivid images, thrilled at the trumpeting and shouts of divinely powerful angels, and, above all, shivered fiercely with fear as rapacious multi-headed beasts rose from the sea and from the earth.

Much of my childhood reading had been random and impressionistic, not purposeful and rationally taken in. The books in our home, an isolated farmhouse over two miles from the nearest neighbor, were all far beyond my years but I read them all anyway, and I lived in a mostly solitary world of fragmented images and Delphic ambiguities, a mental collage of Hiawatha and barrack-room ballads, houyhnhnms and Mohicans, bluebirds and hero-worship, and horses with heads of lions and tails with heads like serpents—the last, of course, from Revelation. For when other reading began to fade in interest, Revelation was always there, as freshly mysterious as ever.

At church I heard sermons on the necessity to watch and pray lest Christ return to earth and find me a slothful servant, or, worse still, a foolish virgin with no oil in my lamp. I heard the warning so often that the Return would occur in a day and hour "when ye think not," that I started making a conscious effort to think about that possibility all the time so as to prevent it. But somehow these rather scary harangues never seemed to me to have any connection with Revelation. I suppose the texts were taken from the Gospels or from Paul rather than from the Apocalypse. Only some years later did I begin to connect the Lamb of Revelation with the Jesus of the Gospels and to realize that the book I considered a pastiche of fantastic images which could be turned to at any odd moment and in no particular sequence was actually a book to be read straight through and to be grappled with intellectually. I went to it not for information, and certainly not for guidance, but for the at once deliciously stimulating and strangely disturbing sensation of leaving the familiar world behind and plunging into a mysterious world of dragons belching seas of water, horses struggling through blood up to their bridles, and angels throwing grapes into a winepress oozing blood while heavenly hosts look on with rejoicing.

Years later on the occasion of that first sermon, however, as an adult who had experienced war first-hand, had read with increasing awareness of structure and theme many more literary works, and had married and become a father, as I stood before a congregation with the Apocalypse open before me, I believed myself ready to interpret the letters to the churches in Revelation if not yet the apocalyptic visions. My choice of one of the letters rather than one of the visions was a compromise of sorts, since the letters include apocalyptic symbols recalled from the inaugural vision and anticipating the final vision of the new heaven and the new earth as well as more matter-of-fact-seeming statements I could apply to the here and now of a local church. I have little memory of that first sermon apart from the text, my concluding exhortation to the hearers to "Remember from whence you have fallen and repent," and, most vividly, the much-too-expensive suit my wife had given me in an effort to make me look like a preacher whether or not I would ever preach like one.

Eight years later, with a master's diploma and an ordination certificate on the wall, I had just resigned my third pastorate when another church invited me to give a series of sermons on the Book of Revelation. Although I was by this time much more confident of my ability to analyze and present expositions of the Bible, I was still intimidated by the prospect of delivering four or five hours of exegesis and application of Revelation over a period of several days. My fascination with the imagery and architectural patterning of the book had grown through the years, but I was still less than intellectually and spiritually comfortable with interpreting Revelation.

The series was never finished. On the fifth night of a planned eight-night series, as I drove through a snow-storm to keep my appointment, I collided head-on with a large truck. A friend with me died immediately, and doctors at first doubted that I would survive. During the ensuing months of hospitalization, images, words, and imaginative extrapolations from the visions and prophecies of Revelation were almost constantly surrounding, filling, elevating and depressing, enlarging and straitening me. I became convinced that my entry into pastoral ministry had been a mistake and that I must correct the error as soon as my health permitted by changing direction from preaching to teaching. I began to plan for graduate school, a doctorate in English, and the career as a teacher-scholar that I have now followed for almost forty years. My own private apocalypse on a highway and a hospital bed had destroyed one world and fashioned another one—if not a New Jerusalem where all tears are wiped away, one which became, for me at least, a world in which God's presence makes a temple, while still desirable, unnecessary.

My few years as a Christian minister, then, were bracketed by an initial and a concluding encounter with the one Bible book that had most charmed and least enlightened me as a boy. On a dean's orders, I began teaching a course in the literary study of the Bible early in my professorial career, but the one book I have continued to avoid including in the syllabus is Revelation—not through distaste for it or fear of its obscurities, but rather through love and reverence for its holy optimism in the face of every reason to despair and for its artistic excellence, both of which far exceed the ability of even the sympathetic critic to describe wholly. In sum, to "explain" it or to "appreciate" it, or especially to anatomize it for homiletical purposes, seemed to me to diminish its holistic effect for me or for the reader. The best the critic can hope for is to produce suggestive analyses that may help to enhance and enlarge the total effect of the Apocalypse for readers, even those whose theological or literary approaches and interpretive conclusions are very different from the critic's. I profited by much that others had written but still did not myself write about or teach Revelation.

Why, then, am I writing about the book now when I have felt inadequate to teach it or write about it for so many years? Because writing an article on the Book of Daniel alone made me realize that Daniel is incomplete without Revelation, and that Revelation depends even more on Daniel than Daniel depends on Ezekiel, Jeremiah, or others of the Hebrew prophets. Having undertaken to write a literary analysis of Daniel, I came to see in the process that I could no more avoid taking the next inevitable step of writing on Revelation than a platform diver can halt his dive before entering the water and ascend to the platform again—such a reversal is possible only in the video camera's instant replay, not in life. The difference is that the diver knows in advance that his commitment in leaving the platform to execute a dive is irreversible, while I did not realize that a kind of literary gravitational attraction would demand that what I started in Daniel must be completed in Revelation.

As for my personal interpretation of the apocalyptic Books of Daniel and Revelation and what the relevance of their message is to Christians, churches, and general readers of today, my biases have doubtless already betrayed themselves, although I have worked at keeping them, if not out of the picture, on the periphery. My beliefs about Revelation are essentially the same as they were almost forty years ago when a highway accident left my series of expositions of the book unfinished. One probable reason for little change in my interpretation is that I deliberately avoided articulating my responses to the interpretations of others until the writing of this book made continued evasion impossible. In any event, my reading, while it has been invaluable in heightening my admiration for the fusion of artistry and passion in the writings of the authors of Daniel and Revelation as well as in increasing my understanding of how the two texts interrelate thematically, has not substantially altered my exegesis and explication of either book from what they were in the 1950s. One could explain this interpretive constancy as stubborn adherence to an ideological pattern superimposed on the text, or as intellectual inertia that resists movement and change even when textual evidence suggests that change is necessary, or as a wish to escape the problems and trials of life in the world by the expectation of an imminent *deus ex machina* that will forever exclude solving problems and enduring trials from human life. Doubtless all these explanations include some germ of truth. But I think the true answer lies in the articulation and reciprocity of meaning between the two texts that are the subject of this book. My instinctive reading of Daniel as historical apocalypse and Revelation as eschatological apocalypse has been confirmed by close study of the two books and of criticism of them.

The summarizing statements I present briefly in this personal afterword are vulnerable to refutation in many of the details, but they seem to me to be true to the substance of Daniel and Revelation taken together. Although I read these texts as a Christian believer, I hope my representations of their combined message are helpful, if only in a very general way, to readers of other faiths or of no faith. Certainly these two books from the past will continue to attract many readers today and in the future apart from the efforts of any one of us who try to understand them for ourselves and express our understanding to others.

The world-system is at its worst essentially anti-God; put another way, even at their best human rulers and governments pursue goals independently of God, goals that are antithetical to the best interests of people who believe in and worship a holy God and take divinely revealed laws and principles seriously enough to give up goods, kindred, and life itself rather than violate them. The young men in the fiery furnace of Babylon, Daniel in the lion's den, John on Patmos, and the two witnesses over whose dead bodies the minions of Revelation's beast-ruler rejoice have such a radical belief in common; while Daniel's central heroes are delivered in life, Revelation's witnesses and other martyrs are delivered only in afterlife. Daniel's prophecy makes provision as well for saints who are not delivered from their trials, or who do not live long enough to participate in the victory Daniel foresees. All of them will awake from the dust of the earth into a life beyond life.

What can break through the perennial cycle of tyranny and oppression, of the callous materialism of the few which neglects the welfare of the many, to establish a just and beneficent world? Daniel presents the stone cut out of a mountain without hands, his Messiah the Prince, to annihilate and replace evil powers; Revelation portrays the King of Kings and Lord of Lords, the Lamb, who both saves the redeemed and destroys in his wrath the evil ones and brings heaven to earth.

But neither book advises believers to adopt a passive, do-nothing stance while they await the breaking into time of God's eternal kingdom. Daniel is to go his way, fulfill his calling, write his book even though part of it is sealed, and his readers are to endure trials before they will possess the kingdom. John is to write and continue to prophesy and the saints are to serve God day and night and, ultimately, reign with Christ. The churches of Asia are to be faithful, do the first work, overcome, strengthen what they have. But Daniel looks forward to an end in a distant future following a long period of historical developments; John assumes that period, except for a short time between reunion with Jesus and earthly judgment, to be already fulfilled. Therefore he portrays an end that must be imminently expected. Even though the wait may be centuries long, the hope of the coming of the risen Lord must be kept fresh. "Surely I come quickly," says Jesus, and John responds immediately, "Even so, come, Lord Jesus."

John himself becomes the prototype of all those who will be caught up to be with the Lord at his coming in his imminent return, just as Daniel is the prototype of those who will sleep in the dust until the time to awake to everlasting life. While Revelation includes glimpses of those who will die and be resurrected, it focuses on the apostle as representative of those who will remain alive for the Return; thus he is elevated above the earth for a heavenly view of the judgment and renewal of the earth. Daniel the book encompasses only those whose future hope will be realized through death and resurrection, and Daniel the man symbolizes them: he will rest and yet stand again at the end of the days. Again, the long look forward towards history's horizon is Daniel's focus, while the expectant look upward is John's, a contrast in perspective reflected, as we have seen, in the structure of the two books.

Although Daniel has an Aramaic section in which the first and the last parts fold back chiastically upon the middle, the thrust of the structure is forward horizontally from narrative to vision with the visions echoing the themes of the narratives. And while Revelation moves forward in accelerating gyres, the whole is arranged in a series of corresponding parallel sections on either side of a visionary and thematic center which seems to rise above and draw into itself both ends, like a spire lifting beholders' eyes towards the sky from which the risen Lord is expected at any time.

Taken together, the two books combine the horizontal, cause-and-effect, linear chain of events that represents the day-to-day and year-to-year life of all human beings with the vertical aspirations, the longed-for transcendental connections between the supernatural and the natural, between God and mankind, those Wordsworthian "intimations of immortality" that carry us forward beyond memories of our origins and lift us upward toward eternity. What Minear says of Revelation can be said of the combined effect of the Book of Daniel and the Apocalypse: they bring thoughtful readers "in touch with an order of reality which transcends space and time by revealing the eternal and universal significance of each day and each place" (278).

> Hence in a season of calm weather
> Though inland far we be,
> Our Souls have sight of that immortal sea
> Which brought us hither,
> Can in a moment travel thither
> And see the Children sport upon the shore,
> And hear the mighty waters rolling evermore.
>
> —William Wordsworth

Unto the place from whence the rivers come, thither they return again.
—Koheleth

Index of Names

Index of Scripture Passages